MISSING

MISSING

A Memoir

CORNELIA MAUDE SPELMAN

JackLeg Press
www.jacklegpress.org
www.corneliaspelman.com

ISBN: 978-1-7375134-4-5

Library of Congress Control Number: 2021948140

This is an authorized reprint of the first edition published by Northwestern
University Press 2010.
www.nupress.northwestern.edu

Chapter 1, "Love, Bill" first appeared in *Chicago* magazine.

All images otherwise not credited are the author's. The names of some
persons in the book have been changed.

Cover design by Richard Every.

For Sam Schneider's great-great-grandchildren—
Leo, Josephine (Poppy), Isaac, and Benjamin, in their hours.

And for Reg.

You have returned, for all of them, for all of their sakes, come to rummage and explore, in your hour, and find a meaning, and a language, and a name.

—William Goyen, *The House of Breath*

CONTENTS

MISSING

PART ONE

My Mother's Story

1

Love, Bill

When I was growing up, I'd heard William Maxwell's name spoken with a respect that Pop reserved for very few people. In the late 1920s, Maxwell and my parents had been part of a literary scene at the University of Illinois at Urbana-Champaign, but I had never met him.

Although the three of them had fallen out of touch some years after college, Pop had followed Maxwell's career at the *New Yorker*, where for forty years he had edited the work of writers such as Eudora Welty, John Updike, Vladimir Nabokov, and John Cheever. "For fiction writers, he was the headquarters," Eudora Welty said of him.

Maxwell, a native of Lincoln, Illinois, was a writer himself—his novels and stories have been republished by the Library of America. His novel *So Long, See You Tomorrow*—described as "rare" and "exquisite"—won a National Book Award in 1982. Pop kept Maxwell's 1934 first novel, *Bright Center of Heaven*, with this note inside it:

> *Did you get my letter? Did Harper's send the book like I told them to? Did Miss Mecker let you review it? What did you say about it? Do you think this is going to be a very Merry Christmas?*
>
> *Billie Maxwell*

5

Mother and Pop remained ravenous readers, though their lives were far away from literary circles. A happy memory from my childhood is of the three of us at home reading in Cincinnati, when the older children were not there. I would be in the blue slipcovered wing chair (I was small enough to curl into it, protected by the wings), Pop lying on the sofa, his pipe in his mouth, Mother in her red armchair next to a big round table piled with stacks of books, the oversize turquoise enamel ashtray filling up with crushed Pall Mall cigarettes as the evening wore on.

Pop had seemed proud of his early friendship with Maxwell, and I had understood, although it was never said, that Maxwell had succeeded, and Pop had not; that Maxwell had entered a larger world that Pop and Mother had aspired to enter also, but that, long before my birth, they had given up as impossible for themselves.

I was the youngest of five children, and by the time I came around, Mother and Pop were worn out. Whatever possibilities there had been for my parents' life belonged to a time before any of us children were born, a time that I pictured as peaceful, free of Pop's quick irritation, of Mother's incessant smoker's cough—when they were young and newly married, just out of college, still pals with Maxwell.

In 1984, ten years after Mother had finally smoked herself to death, when Pop was seriously ill, my husband, Reg, needed to contact Maxwell about an anthology of Chicago writers. I suggested, "Tell him you're married to Norman and Elizabeth Spelman's daughter." Maxwell's response had been an invitation to tea on our upcoming trip to New York from our home in Evanston, Illinois.

Reg and I rang his doorbell in a building on the Upper East Side, where he and his wife, Emmy, had lived for many years. I was thirty-seven at the time, older by far than he, Pop, and Mother had been when they had been friends at the University of Illinois.

The door to his apartment opened. "How you look like your mother and father!" he exclaimed at once. He was a small, dignified man with lively brown eyes. His apartment was light and spacious, filled with books. His spotlessly polished windows framed a view of the East River. "Just cleaned this week," he told me, smiling, when I commented on them.

We had arrived a bit early and felt awkward, and we followed him into the kitchen, where he was still making tea. Emmy was away preparing her first exhibition of paintings.

Bill didn't speak rapidly, allowing more silences than most people do, and providing, I thought, an equivalent to white space on a page of writing. This could have the effect of making someone rush in to fill the quiet. I pressed my lips together. I felt a loyalty to my parents, a responsibility to represent them well, to not say the wrong thing.

Bill turned to me from the cupboard where he was seeking tea cookies. "Your father was a very handsome man, you know, one of the best-looking men on campus." This surprised me. At that time, I was just old enough to understand that my father had lived so much of his life without me as his daughter.

"Was he?" I replied. "Was he a ladies' man?"

Bill was thoughtful, arranging cookies on a plate. After a moment he turned and said, "No. I don't think very handsome men have to be. Do you?"

Reg brushed my hand with his, to indicate that he liked the way Bill spoke. The sun was pouring in through the kitchen window on this elderly man, on his white hair and almost translucent skin. "Of course he's old," I thought. "He's my father's age, seventy-six." Yet Bill's face retained a puckish charm, and a few minutes later, seated in the living room, as he was pouring our tea, I said, "You have such a young face! I think you were a mischievous boy; perhaps you are still mischievous!" Something about his face and his brown eyes made me think of a boy I had known in school, smaller than I, always ready to be my ally in pranks or games to relieve our boredom, and usually the one to be caught and punished for what I, a proper little girl and therefore unsuspected, had initiated.

Bill regarded me, and I was briefly afraid I'd been impolite. "You see, it's odd," he began after a moment of thought. "One

7

gets older and yet feels the same inside. I find it a shock to see myself in the mirror, to see that I am somehow in this old man's body."

Pop had recently said the same thing to me, not long before what had turned out to be a brain tumor had erased such thoughts from his mind, turning him into a blank, sweet child.

"I enjoy life so much," Bill continued. "I have no regrets — except that so many of my friends have died, or are ill. I'm not ready to die. I don't want to miss the rest of the party."

"I'm glad!" I said. "You have no sense, then, that the party has ended for you?"

"Oh, no, not at all. I just realize that my body is getting very old," he replied.

"I'm afraid the party has ended for my father. I'm sorry to tell you that he's very ill right now," I said.

Bill shook his head and put his teacup down on the table. His hand trembled a little.

"This is so hard for me to believe," he said. "I remember him only as a young man, you see."

I thought of a photograph I loved, one taken a few years after my parents had graduated. It showed their first apartment — a studio, Mother had called it once — a description I liked because I associated it with artists. Mother was wearing a softly draped dress and a necklace of long beads. Her hair was swept to one side like a 1930s movie star's. Pop was sitting in a large armchair, a pipe in his mouth, his thick dark hair tousled. He looked like an impossibly young version of the father I knew.

We all sat quietly.

"Your father was a journalist, was he not?" Bill asked me. I understood suddenly why Pop had never renewed contact with his old friend, why he had simply kept him in sight from afar, all these years.

"Oh, no. He would have liked to be a writer, or a college professor. He did write book reviews for the *Kansas City Star* for a while after college. No, he worked selling dials and nameplates for a manufacturing company."

My voice or manner must have betrayed my reluctance to

Pop at the University of Illinois, circa 1928

Pop and Mother's studio apartment, Kansas City, Missouri, circa 1932

reveal my father's failure. Bill sensed it at once, and was kind. "In a good novel one doesn't look for a success story," he said, "but for a story that moves one with its human drama and richness of experience."

Grateful, I went on. "My parents' life went off track somewhere. They got bogged down, with the children. Mother, too, wanted a bigger life. She loved reading and wrote a book manuscript herself once, a book about religion, but I don't know what happened to it."

"It would be interesting to read it, don't you think?" he asked me. "You might learn a lot about her, reading her book."

"Cornelia was hoping you could tell her something about her mother," Reg said.

"She died ten years ago," I explained. "And she was sick for many years before that. She ended up in such a sad way."

Bill nodded and murmured, "I'm so sorry." He was silent for a moment.

"Well," he said, "your mother was great fun; she laughed a lot and was very witty. Did you find her witty?"

"Oh, yes," I said. "She was very funny." Though later, when I tried to think of funny things she had said, I realized her humor was self-deprecating and ironic, often dark, especially after she was sick. The humor of the prisoner or victim.

Bill continued, "She was brilliantly different and generally admired. More vivid than other girls—the way certain tropical birds are vivid. And while I can't say she was beautiful—not like you—you're beautiful, with her eyes and your father's bones— she was enchanting."

I smiled at him. I'd heard he was a charming man.

He told me that he and my parents had met at the University of Illinois through a sorority sister of Mother's. "There was a small group of like-minded people—no more than enough to fill the kitchen of the sorority house," Bill said, "who formed a rather literary group. In a college largely made up of engineering and agriculture students, the group felt—to me, I mean— aristocratic.

"The girls were all beautiful and saw no reason to hide

the fact that they were intelligent. I was half in love with half a dozen of them. The boys were the boys they were dating. I don't remember any that were not physically attractive. Your father was the most attractive of all. He was not only handsome, he was unpredictable, wildly amusing, and like no one else. Your mother, too."

I waited, and he added, after a moment, "But I can't think of any stories about her, really. I'm sorry if I disappoint you."

He did recall a story about Pop, however. Once, after a tea party at the home of one of Mother's sorority sisters, the hostess had acted haughty because Pop had used the wrong fork. Later, telling Bill about her reaction, Pop had stuttered, "Y-y-you'd th-th-think I'd t-t-taken out m-m-my p-p-pecker and wh-wh-whammed it on the gr-gr-grand p-p-piano!" We laughed together.

Bill's tea was excellent, smoky and delicate. I had never tasted tea like it. He was impeccably courteous, and in his presence I wanted to be equally polite, so, although I wished to talk with him longer, after an hour I felt we should go. He helped me on with my coat. I wished to embrace him, but for some reason I held back.

"I hope I will see you again," he said to us at the door, and then closed it, extinguishing suddenly the lovely light from his clean windows.

Although I visited Bill and Emmy in New York only a few more times over the years, I wrote to him, sharing my thoughts and feelings about Mother and Pop and about my own life, sometimes sending along brief excerpts from Mother's diaries or letters because I was trying to understand and write about what had happened to that girl he had described as "vivid."

With his perfect courtesy, he always replied. I wondered, later, if I'd ended up asking more of him than he'd bargained for when he'd invited us to tea. But he had written to me " 'Only connect,' Mr. Forster said, and this we have never failed to do" and as an inscription in one of his books, "For Cornelia Spelman, whom I loved at first sight."

His affection emboldened me to imagine him as the parent

Mother in 1927, shortly before she went to the University of Illinois

Pop, Mother, and friends at the University of Illinois, circa 1929;
the back of the photograph carries the inscription,
"Remember gin and lime juice?"

—both father and mother—I wished I'd had, and to turn to him at times for guidance. His two daughters, years after his death, when asked what he was like as a father, spoke of their disappointments. But as Emmy once said to me, during a visit, when I was telling them about my parents' failings, "Sometimes people make great friends but not great parents."

Bill not only was a link to Mother's past, when she had been young and healthy, but, like her, he had experienced the death of a parent when he was a child. His mother had died in January 1919, of the Spanish influenza, when he was ten, and Mother's father had died of a ruptured appendix in November 1918, when she was seven.

Bill had written about his mother's death in several of his novels, and when in *So Long, See You Tomorrow*, he described what it had been like for him, it was as if he were speaking, too, for what Mother as a child must have felt:

> The worst that could happen had happened, and the shine went out of everything. . . . Between the way things used to be and the way they were now was a void that couldn't be crossed. . . . I hadn't gone anywhere and nothing was changed, so far as the roof over our heads was concerned, it was just that she was in the cemetery.

When they were friends at the University of Illinois, Bill didn't know that Mother, too, had lost a parent. They had never talked about it. At that time, Mother seemed to be thriving. Bill, however, was not.

In his novel *The Folded Leaf*, the main character is a university student named Lymie whose mother's death when he was a child has left him needing "more than the ordinary amount of love."

Lymie becomes close friends with another student, Spud, the only close relationship he's had since his mother died. But because of a misunderstanding, Spud turns against him. Lymie's response is to swallow iodine and cut his throat and wrists.

I wrote Bill to ask if this had happened to him. He replied,

*My novel is a mixture of autobiography and invention,
but the three main characters and their relations to each
other are all taken from life, and so are the details of the
suicide attempt. I don't know which is worse, clinical
depression or a broken heart, but in my case it was the
second. I didn't so much wish that I was dead, as not
want to go on living in a world where the truth (or what
I thought was the truth) had no power to make itself
believed. I also felt a conscious desire to go where my
mother was and to be with her, being still enough of a
child to believe, to half believe anyway, that this was
possible.*

I asked him what my parents had known of this. He replied,

*I am sure that your father and mother knew that I had
tried to commit suicide but how much else they knew
I have no idea. I wore a turtle neck sweater, the only
one on campus, until the scar had healed, so I wasn't
exactly inconspicuous. My friends were very supporting,
and never mentioned the suicide or asked any questions.
When I still had bandages on my throat I went to a
dance at the Theta house and the girls saw to it that I
had a lovely time.*

Though he survived, of course, he continued to suffer. He
wrote me that in order to avoid being hurt again by his friend,

*I walked about twenty-five feet away and made myself
stop loving him. The price for this was that I couldn't
love anyone else for a long long time. I went into analysis
because I felt that what was happening to me was what
happens to a tree when you cut the center branch out.*

Bill's psychoanalyst in New York was Theodor Reik, who had
been a student of Sigmund Freud. During one of my visits with
Bill, he told me about the session with Reik in which he had
finally returned to his grief at his mother's death. In *So Long,
See You Tomorrow*, he had written this same scene he had told
me about:

16

After six months of lying on an analyst's couch . . . I relived that nightly pacing, with my arm around my father's waist. From the living room into the front hall, then, turning, past the grandfather's clock and on into the library, and from the library into the living room. From the library into the dining room, where my mother lay in her coffin. Together we stood looking down at her. I meant to say to the fatherly man who was not my father, the elderly Viennese, another exile, with thick glasses and a Germanic accent, I meant to say *I couldn't bear it*, but what came out of my mouth was "I can't bear it." This statement was followed by a flood of tears such as I hadn't ever known before, not even in my childhood.

I saw Bill for the last time in the late spring of 2000. I knew it would be the last. Illness had kept him in and out of hospitals for months. Although I had written ahead to ask whether he would be well enough to see me, and phoned upon my arrival in New York, still, when I arrived at his door at the appointed time, it wasn't his wife, Emmy, who opened it but a tall, dignified woman, unknown to me—a housekeeper or nurse. Bill had spent the previous night in the hospital, but, she insisted, she would wake him.

I sat down on the sofa and looked around at this room, where I had been on every visit, and gazed out the clean windows. In a few moments I heard a raspy "Cornelia!" and turned to see Bill, in his plaid flannel bathrobe, on the tall woman's arm. Beaming at me, he raised both arms for an embrace.

At ninety-one, he looked both ancient and very young. I thought of "Bunny," the mother's name for her beloved little boy, her "angel child" in his novel *They Came Like Swallows*.

We embraced, and I helped him to the sofa. His breathing was rapid and shallow, like a puppy's. I would have only a few minutes with him.

"I want to see you tell your mother's story," Bill whispered— he couldn't speak in his old voice. "It seems it would even it out, somehow, for what happened to her." I pressed his gnarly hand.

I knew he would not be around long enough to know if I had completed it.

"Bill," I said, "I've been reading the books of Thich Nhat Hanh, a Vietnamese Buddhist monk."

He nodded, whispering, "I know of him."

"And thinking about how when we die we change form," I said.

After a pause, Bill whispered, "If I could come back in another form, I think it would be as sunshine." He smiled gently.

"Then, whenever I feel the sun on my face, I will think of you," I told him. "You will always be with me, Bill. Because of all I have felt for you, and all I have learned from you."

He smiled. "When you feel the sun, then, you'll think of me?"

"Yes. I will."

The tall woman came back into the room to return him to bed. We embraced. As they walked slowly down the hall away from me, I let myself out the door.

One fall, several years before he died, Bill had written me, from his and Emmy's summer home in Yorktown Heights:

> It's a gray day, maybe rain tonight, and everywhere a feeling of one thing ending and another beginning. The last of the peaches, and at the vegetable stand all the flowers and baskets of tomatoes removed in order to make room for pumpkins and squashes of the genteel ornamental kind. In about ten days we will be moving back to the city and the cat can no longer ask to be let in and out sixty times a day.
>
> Don't—or at least I don't think it is reasonable to— feel sad about the transitoriness of things. What you have had you will always have if you are a rememberer.
>
> Love, Bill

2

Betrayals

In the summer of 1973, before Mother got too sick to drive, she taped a handwritten sign—made from several pieces of the cardboard that came inside Pop's laundered shirts—to the bumper of her little, dented, blue Ford Falcon, listing the number of American soldiers killed in Vietnam each week.

Despite the honks, shouts, and uplifted middle fingers her sign attracted on the street or in the parking lots of the supermarket, the Laundromat, and the library, her main destinations in Plymouth, Massachusetts, the small seaside town to which she and Pop and I had moved in 1962, she kept it up.

Outraged by the war, Mother wrote many letters to President Nixon, to congressmen, and to newspapers; one she sent to the editor of the *Boston Herald-Traveler*—which didn't publish it—read:

> *Gentlemen: Certainly those who promote and attend a
> rally backing the Vietnam war are entitled to do so, but I
> object strenuously to the statement, made repeatedly and
> on television, that the Wakefield rally was composed of
> "those who back our troops in Vietnam," thus implying
> that those of us who oppose the Administration policy are
> somehow against our own troops. On the contrary, we are
> so heartily for our own troops (and for the country and*

*for our world) that we believe the best way to back them
is to remove them as rapidly as possible. We are not anti-
troops, we are anti-war.*

Mother despised Nixon. The only letter of her many to the White House that had ever been acknowledged was one she had written in jest, praising the new, quasi-royal uniforms Nixon had ordered for the White House guard. She had posted the reply, a gold-edged, engraved card, thanking her for her "confidence and understanding," on her kitchen funny board.

She wrote my oldest sister, who lived in Amsterdam,

*I've had plenty to watch on the tube—I stay glued to
Watergate, which has now of course passed all ordinary
belief. I'm sure that a year ago any self-respecting
publisher would have turned down any manuscript
describing the happenings as being so fanciful as to be
silly. But I think that sonofabitch in the White House is
going to get away with it, and finish out his term.*

Pop claimed that Mother's fury at Watergate was "p-p-pro-longing her l-l-life."

By that summer of 1973, Mother had already been ill for eight years with emphysema, which had reduced her slender, elegant body of 125 pounds to an emaciated 90. She was only sixty-two, but her skin was as wrinkled as if she were ninety-two. Her skeletal arms were marked with bruises caused by her illness, and the veins on both sides of her neck were distended from her constant effort to breathe.

She'd been reliant on continual oxygen for the past year, and had in her nose a green rubber catheter that tethered her to ugly green metal oxygen tanks. Her nose seemed to have grown larger as the rest of her face had shrunk. Only her large, bright, intelligent eyes, hazel and almond shaped, had remained the same.

In addition to big oxygen tanks by her bed, she had a portable tank that permitted her to move about, and she was still capable of cooking dinner at night. Sometimes she and Pop would go out to eat at Bert's, a nearby seafood restaurant, or she would play bridge with a few women from her new church. A life-long Episcopalian, Mother had recently converted to Roman Catholicism. The sicker she got, the stronger the magic she needed.

Always a great reader, and briefly a graduate student in English (the one course she had completed before leaving school to marry Pop had been Tragedy I), she still checked out piles of cellophane-covered mystery novels each week from the Plymouth library, a small, white clapboard building on a steep, narrow street overlooking the water. Although she owned shelves of books about theology (*The Problem of Pain, City of God, God's Plan on Salvation*), in the last few years of her illness, Mother's reading had narrowed to her beloved thrillers and the newspaper.

Because of the weight of her large oxygen tanks, and because she could no longer climb the narrow flight of stairs to the bedroom she and Pop used to share, Mother was living in a room on the first floor, adjacent to the kitchen.

This room and a bath had been added on to the house a few years earlier. Pop's ninety-year-old mother, Gran, had paid for the construction so that she could live with Pop and Mother and be near her other son, Pop's younger brother, a doctor, who also lived in Plymouth.

But Gran was in the room only a year. Her sighing, humming, and denture clicking were getting on Mother's nerves; then Gran began accusing Mother and Pop of hiding things from her. But Gran was the one who was hiding things—raw chicken disappeared from the refrigerator, and several days later, when the putrid smell of decomposition led Mother to it, she found it stuffed into Gran's clothes hamper.

When Gran became convinced that the optometrist she had visited had removed her eyeballs and replaced them upside down, Mother and Pop moved her to Mayflower House, a nearby nursing home. Mother felt guilty about putting the old lady there. It seemed merciful when, after a few months, and after being put into a straitjacket, Gran died.

After Gran went into Mayflower House, Mother moved into her room. It was furnished with the few things Gran had brought with her from her apartment in Hartford, Connecticut—a tall, dark wooden dresser and matching single bed; a faded blue velvet sofa; a coffee table that Mother covered with books and crossword puzzles; and by the window—which, if you stood close to it and turned your head to the left, had a view of the ocean—a gold upholstered chair, soon torn to shreds by Mother's cats, Ben and Peachy.

The small, yellow clapboard house, near the beach, had been built as a summer cottage, and the scale of the rooms was small, almost dollhouse-like. A narrow stairway led up from the living room to a landing illuminated by a small, square stained-glass window, and another few stairs took you up to the second floor, where there were a bathroom and four small bedrooms, each large enough to hold only a bed, nightstand, and dresser.

Mother had made the house pleasant and cozy when we had first moved there from Cincinnati in 1962. She had sewn crisp white and gold curtains; had hung the Picasso, Modigliani, and Van Gogh prints that had been in our other houses; and, as always, had arranged spots for reading and smoking. She had tucked the worn red wing chair in by the fireplace, next to a round wooden table with a fat cream-colored pottery lamp and her large turquoise ashtray. The walnut secretary that had been passed down to her from her grandmother in Iowa was polished and tidy, and in it she kept her stamps in a round brass holder.

But in 1967, after her mother, Cornie, died, Mother replaced our furniture with Cornie's, which had fit her mansion but didn't fit our cottage. The dining room looked crowded with a heavy polished wood table and fancy chairs with leather backs and gold satin tassels. The living room was jammed with a long rose velvet sofa, satin upholstered armchairs, and a mahogany organ that no one played. Heavy floral drapes, too long for the small windows, dragged on the floor.

Mother hung a crucifix in each room. Beneath the kitchen crucifix was a framed drawing of a low, stone entranceway, like that of an ancient building in Bethlehem, with the verse,

So little is the door!
Stoop low; all else must go.
But oh! How much they win
Who enter in.

It was in her one room off the kitchen that Mother spent most of her time. Next to her bed were the tall green oxygen tanks and a small oak table with two drawers. In the top drawer, she kept packages of narrow black cigarillos and matches and in the bottom drawer an ashtray.

Mother must have bought them herself, when she was still driving, and the store clerk must have rolled her eyes at the sight of this woman, tethered to oxygen, still buying smokes. After Mother was confined to home, Pop, then my oldest brother, Frank, must have bought them for her.

She had always smoked unfiltered Pall Malls. Maybe she had switched to cigarillos thinking she would smoke less. Or maybe the cigarillos' dark tobacco and gold-trimmed boxes made her think of European cigarettes, and my oldest sister in Amsterdam.

Anyone in the kitchen could see into her room.

I was twenty-seven, already divorced, and living with my three-year-old son, Sam, in New Hampshire, where I had a job as a secretary at a small ad agency. I drove down to see Mother every month or two.

If I was in the kitchen washing the dishes or cooking, I could see into her room as she furtively lit a cigarillo, grabbed a few puffs off it, then stubbed it out in the ashtray and closed the drawer. Wisps of smoke continued to curl out of the closed drawer, but I pretended I didn't see.

Not that anyone would have to see to know she was smoking, because the cigarillos smelled awful, especially when they had been lit and stubbed out again.

I had given up saying anything to Mother about her smoking. I had pleaded with Pop to put her into a hospital as you would with a drug addict, but he didn't.

Until Mother's first hospitalization eight years earlier, when her lungs had been washed out with ether—a horrendous treatment—she had smoked from the minute she woke up until the time she went to sleep.

In the mornings, sitting on the side of her bed in one of her sheer, sleeveless nylon nightgowns, she would shake a Pall Mall out of its deep red pack and light up. At night, she would read and smoke in bed until she turned out the lamp. The smell of tobacco smoke and the sound of her loose, phlegmy cough had been the smell and sound of my childhood. When Mother attended my school play, I could hear her cough from backstage.

The ether procedure and the diagnosis of emphysema had initially shocked her into attending a smoking cessation class, and she had managed to stop, for one month. But then she resumed smoking almost as much as she had before. Pop, a steady smoker of pipes, cigars, and cigarettes, frequently said he was going to stop "when the w-w-weather g-g-got b-b-better," but he never had.

Mother inherited some money, as well as furniture, when her mother died, and so she was able, for the first time, to travel to Amsterdam to see my oldest sister.

My sister's friends, writers and artists, were high-spirited and heavy-drinking, and Mother tried to keep up with them. In a photo from one party, Mother, a drink in one hand and a cigarette in the other, sits next to a young man who is naked except for a tie.

In Venice, a painter friend pushed Mother around in a wheelchair, a cigarillo hanging from her mouth, her lap filling with flowers he bought her from the stalls. They laughed uproariously when he raced her wheelchair up to the canals as if to push her in—as uproariously as her damaged lungs permitted.

But then, within a few years, Mother became too ill to return to Europe. She was in and out of the hospital. Of what use were the antibiotics, the expectorants, the inhalers, the treatments with postural drainage, the intermittent positive-pressure breathing device, when she continued to smoke? As time passed and she only declined, it became clear that Mother was going to die from emphysema—it was just a question of when.

Pop, sixty-five, didn't have a job or retirement income. We had never had enough money. We had moved within Cincinnati three times, each move to a less expensive house, then an apartment. One of our houses had a large hole in the kitchen linoleum, and its upstairs rooms were missing doorknobs, so you'd have to borrow a doorknob from one room to get into another.

I don't know why Pop didn't fix the doorknobs or the floor, since he considered himself a handyman. One Thanksgiving, while working to reattach the back stair banister, his electric drill went through the wall of the kitchen, spewing sawdust into the turkey Mother was preparing.

For a long time, Pop had been employed as a salesman by a manufacturing company owned by Cornie's second husband, but he had finally been let go. While his boss hadn't considered Pop "so crooked you'd have to screw him into the ground," as he described another employee, Pop's lack of attention to work was notable. He'd once forgotten to put on the hand brake in the new company car, and it had rolled into the Ohio River. His boss said Pop "wasn't a bad salesman, he just wasn't interested in it." Pop, he judged, wished that he were a college professor but "wasn't willing to put in the work to be one."

The reason Mother, Pop, and I had moved to Plymouth in my junior year of high school was that Pop had a new job. He was happy about the move—he was from Hartford, and his younger brother lived in Plymouth.

But for Mother, the move meant leaving St. Michael and All Angels, the Episcopal church where she had been working for racial integration, and becoming the new member of a conservative and decidedly all-white church; and for me, it meant leaving my school and friends.

But then Pop's job hadn't worked out after all. Since Mother was too sick to work any longer as a medical secretary, they were living on her Social Security disability checks and the small dividends from Cornie's estate.

To earn money, Pop got the idea to make archival-quality boxes for rare books, a highly skilled craft about which he knew nothing. He thought he was good with his hands—he reminded us that his father had been a dentist and his grandfather a watchmaker. He hired a young man to dig out wheelbarrows full of dirt to enlarge the small basement under the Plymouth cottage, and he crammed the low-ceilinged, pipe-threaded area full of quaint used book-box equipment.

Although Pop said he had orders from several universities and libraries, he didn't finish many boxes. He said that he couldn't get any work done because he needed to take care of Mother and the house.

The house was a mess.

Rain had leaked into the part of the porch Pop had enclosed for storage—Mother called it the futility room—and ruined part of her grandmother's walnut desk. Stacks of mail and newspapers cluttered the kitchen, dirty laundry piled up on top of the washing machine, and the cat box filled the downstairs with the smell of ammonia. The cats had torn up Cornie's satin upholstered chairs and her rose velvet sofa, which was also stained with drool from Pop's fawn boxer, Nicky.

Pop had a habit of getting dogs without consulting Mother. His previous dog, a black Lab mix, had to be given away when she bit a visitor. Nicky didn't bite, but he once had a wet dream under the dining room table during a dinner party. He was known to stop at the cat box, eat cat turds, vomit, and then eat the vomit.

Pop let him run loose. Nicky regularly overturned garbage cans at the nearby beach, and the beach patrol complained. Nicky and the cats roamed outside, bringing in fleas, and fur floated about Mother's room, which was supposed to be kept free of dust and pollution.

Then, in July, my oldest brother, Frank, came from Michigan for a visit. Pop wrote me (long-distance phone calls were rare in those days) that Frank was going to move in with them.

I didn't really know Frank. He was eleven years older than I, and there were two sisters and a brother between us. By the time I was eight, he had already left home.

A little shorter than Pop's six feet, two inches, Frank didn't have Pop's languid, tall grace, but he was handsome. He had high cheekbones, a strong, straight nose, sparkly hazel eyes, and dark, wavy hair.

Frank didn't stutter like Pop, but he laughed nervously after nearly everything he said. His voice was so constricted it sounded as if he had inhaled helium. He blinked rapidly and constantly smoked.

Pop had saved many of our childhood drawings and school papers—as well as copies of his own letters—and in first grade I had drawn a picture of us five children, with Frank as far away from me as possible. I had colored all of his clothes black.

My oldest sister told me that Frank had always lied about everything, even little things that wouldn't have gotten him in trouble. He had been expelled from high school for stealing money from an organization of which he was the treasurer. Although he managed to get into college, he quickly flunked out.

My oldest sister said that Pop had beaten Frank. She especially remembered one occasion when he had dragged Frank into the basement and beaten him with a belt while Mother stood silently at the kitchen sink, washing the same dishes over and over. Pop had beaten my oldest sister, too, sometimes chasing her up the stairs with a belt in his hand.

Mother once told me that, before I was born, Pop had hit a dog of theirs so hard that he had accidentally killed it. Yet she didn't connect Frank's problems with Pop's violence. Frank had been very sick as a child with encephalitis, a brain inflammation, and she said that he had never been the same afterward.

When I was ten, and Frank was twenty-one, after he had been living with a roommate in an apartment and working for a couple of years, he married a pretty girl with a slender waist, light brown hair, and a sweet smile.

All the relatives came to Cincinnati for the wedding.

Gran came, bringing her extra wig in a hatbox. I crept into her room to look at the coifed silver hair lying on tissue paper.

*My drawing, circa 1952, of Frank (far left),
my three other siblings, and me (far right)*

Cornie came, too. I had been named in her honor, and my baptismal certificate stated that her duty as my godmother was to pray for me:

> Watch over my godchild Cornelia, O Lord, as her days increase, bless and guide her wherever she may be . . . strengthen her when she stands, comfort her when discouraged or sorrowful, raise her up if she falls.

This was the first time I remembered ever meeting her.

Mother said of her, "She likes things better than people." But I treasured seeing "our" name, written in her graceful handwriting, in the children's books she sent me for my birthday and Christmas.

Pop took home movies of the big dinner Mother hosted the night before the wedding. Though overall his movies were of such poor quality that, years later, my middle sister gave them ratings of B (black), MB (mostly black), and OOF (out of focus), this movie was pretty good. It showed seventy-five-year-old Cornie smiling pleasantly, her white teeth gleaming in her large wet mouth. Her thin brown hair was pulled up into a bun. She was wearing pearl earrings, a pearl choker around her wattled neck, a large diamond ring, and a diamond watch. Her swollen feet overflowed the tops of her sleek wine-colored leather heels.

Her sister, my great-aunt Maude, a year younger than Cornie, sat next to her on the sofa, a drink and cigarette in her hand. She, too, was wearing a pearl choker around her wattled neck. She made a face at the camera and laughed.

Pop's sister and brother and their spouses, a cousin I would never meet again, the bride's parents, Frank and the bride, Gran, Cornie and Maude, my sisters and my other brother and I are all shown moving around the dining room table helping ourselves to the fragrant roast beef and Yorkshire pudding that were Mother's specialties. I had helped to set that dining table with a white lace cloth, the flowered purple-and-rose Spode china, and the pearl-handled silver knives that had belonged to Cornie and Maude's mother.

Mother, very animated, talking and laughing, her mouth moving silently in the old movie, an apron over her dress, was wearing sparkly earrings. She stood to the side of the table, a cigarette in her hand, making sure that everyone was getting what they needed. After dinner, Maude, who was said to have entertained the troops overseas in the Great War, vigorously played our upright piano with a cigarette hanging out of her mouth, her eyes flashing, and the loose skin under her chin swinging— my middle sister and I screamed with excitement.

For the wedding at St. Michael and All Angels the next day, I got to wear a new blue-flowered dress and shoes with little heels. The little glass eyes of the minks linked together feet to mouth in Cornie's fur stole stared at me from the pew ahead.

According to the newspaper's wedding announcement, the bride's headband of velvet "held her fingertip-length veil of illusion." Pop's movie of the wedding reception in the parish hall shows the bridesmaids' autumnal ruby, yellow, and green puffy taffeta dresses, and Frank laughing as he lifts the cuffs of his trousers to show off green striped socks. A cigarette burns in his hand.

Pop's movie from ten months later shows Mother, my middle sister, and me outside a hospital door crowding up to Frank's wife as she emerges with their baby in her arms.

But one morning, soon after his son's first birthday, Frank left for work and didn't come back. His wife discovered that he had stuffed the telephone receiver with cotton to mute the bell, apparently afraid that she would get calls about the thousand-dollar loan he had secretly taken out and the debts he had left her. She discovered that he had been fired from his job weeks earlier and had only been pretending to go to work.

The stamped and addressed thank-you notes for baby presents she had given to Frank to mail a year earlier were discovered stuffed into a cupboard.

Pop, with the help of the police, located Frank in another part of Ohio and persuaded him to come back. But on the day he had promised to return, a telegram arrived:

Mother's Iowa grandmother's Spode china
and mother-of-pearl and silver knife

I MISSED AGAIN IF YOU CAN FIND IT IN YOUR HEART TO
FORGIVE ME I HOPE YOU WILL AM SORRY I'M NOT ABLE
TO ACCEPT RESPONSIBILITY BUT BY THE TIME YOU
RECEIVE THIS WIRE I WILL BE IN ST. LOUIS ALL GOOD LUCK
TO YOU AND LITTLE FRANK.

Could encephalitis damage someone's conscience?

Some months later, a woman in Olney, Illinois, called Frank's wife. She had found a suitcase by the side of the highway with Frank's name and his old address and phone number in it, as well as receipts for T-shirts, socks, underwear, and work clothes. But no one knew where he had gone.

At some point, later on, Pop got a phone call from a Texas rancher who had employed Frank, thought highly of him, and was worried because Frank had disappeared. But Pop had given up trying to find him.

Frank's wife recalled that he had always admired Richard Halliburton, an adventurer who had traveled the world and disappeared trying to cross the Pacific in his Chinese sailing ship, the *Sea Dragon*.

Frank had been missing for two years when Mother and Pop were contacted by an Episcopalian priest who had befriended Frank at a soup kitchen and persuaded him to get treatment for alcoholism. Frank was in the Mendocino State Hospital—originally called the Mendocino State Asylum for the Insane—near Ukiah, California.

His wife traveled by bus all the way from Cincinnati to see him. They made plans to resume their life together, and he promised to send Little Frank a big toy truck. But when he was discharged from the hospital, instead of coming home, he disappeared again.

His wife moved in with her mother and went back to nursing school. Years later, she learned that her mother had written Cornie, asking for financial help, but Cornie had never replied.

Some years passed. Frank's wife had obtained a divorce; Mother and Pop and I had moved from Cincinnati to Plymouth. No one talked about Frank.

I was away at college when Mother got a phone call from a woman who said she was Frank's wife. Feeling sorry for Mother, she had persuaded Frank to let her call. Mother was overjoyed. In a letter, she quoted to me from the parable of the prodigal son: "For this, my son, was dead, and is alive again; he who was lost, is found." She had never before revealed to me her feelings about his disappearance.

Frank's first wife, who by then had remarried, wanted her husband to adopt Little Frank. Mother, acting as intermediary, sent on to her the letter Frank wrote in response to the adoption request:

> *After much consideration, and Mother's letter, and*
> *your subsequent call to her, I am writing to say that*
> *I'm fine, and to thank you and your husband for your*
> *undeserved consideration in asking for my permission*
> *to adopt your son.*
>
> *Where shall I proceed in this letter to you? Other*
> *than to say that I have been most fortunate in travel-*
> *ing, and fortunate in finding a wife who enjoyed travel,*
> *and who let us run until it became futile to go anymore.*
> *We have been in my wife's hometown for about a year*
> *and one-half, both of us are working, and enjoy our jobs.*
>
> *Perhaps I am trying to say that at thirty-one I*
> *have found a maturity that I lacked ten years ago,*
> *and am reasonably content with life as it is without*
> *having to try to change everything to suit myself.*
>
> *If I continue this letter, I shall probably become*
> *rather vague and mundane. Thank you again,*
> *for your good wishes, and for your consideration.*
> *Have a very happy holiday season and my best to*
> *all of you.*

Frank and his second wife visited Mother and Pop several times, but then, after a few years, they, too, got divorced. Frank quickly married again, but the marriage lasted only a few months, and my parents never met that wife.

Pop told me that Frank had stolen each of his wives' savings by persuading them to put their money into a joint account with him. He said that Frank had been caught embezzling money from the restaurant he had been managing, but his boss liked him so much he wouldn't press charges if Frank paid him back.

Frank was going to move in with Mother and Pop, get a job, and help Pop take care of Mother and the house.

Three months after Frank moved in, Pop wrote to say that Mother had accused Frank of trying to kill her. Pop wrote that the doctor thought it might be the result of a drug she had been taking. She had refused to do anything Pop or Frank asked her to, so Pop took her to the emergency room.

After some days in the hospital, it was decided—although I didn't know who decided it, Pop or the doctors—that Mother would not return home but would, instead, go into that same nursing home in which Gran had died.

Although I felt a little frightened by Mother's accusation, since Pop didn't take it seriously, I didn't either. Although my oldest sister had told me of Pop's violence toward Frank and her, he hadn't—except for a few spankings—hit us three younger children.

I had enjoyed Pop's sense of fun. When I got bored in Sunday church, Pop, sitting beside me in the pew, would turn to me, wink, and, taking my hand in his, pretend to unscrew each finger, making me giggle. Sometimes on weekends when he and Mother listened to records of New Orleans jazz, he would dance. His eyes snapping, he would perform a sliding and hopping step, elbows akimbo, that made us laugh.

As I got older, he suggested books to me. "I think you'd like this, kid; this is fine writing," he would say, giving me Willa Cather's collected works, bound in faded green cloth, which he had found at a used bookstore.

His face lit up when he saw me, and on my eighteenth birthday card he had written: "For my dear youngest one, who is surrounded by brightness—may your gentleness and honesty be met with love all your life." If he put Mother in a nursing home, it must be because it was the best place for her to be.

I went to see Mother as soon as I could, taking with me three-year-old Sam, who shrank back against me as the nursing home residents, who had been frozen in their wheelchairs in attitudes of dejection and despair, came to life at the sight of him, reaching out to touch him with their pale, bony, hands. Beneath the odor of disinfectant and institutional food was the faint smell of urine.

Mother, on tranquilizers and antipsychotic drugs, seemed as if she were looking at us from the wrong end of a telescope. She didn't repeat her accusation about Frank, and I didn't refer to it. She even expressed gratitude that Frank was there to keep Pop company.

But as it turned out, Pop had found company.

As soon as Frank had moved in, Pop left on a car trip. He visited me in New Hampshire and my middle sister in Massachusetts, then went to Vermont to stay for several days with Mother's friend from church in Cincinnati, Louise, who had separated from her rich husband and moved into their vacation home.

Mother had told me earlier that spring that Louise had visited them. She had cooked dinner, set the table with a pretty tablecloth no one had seen for years, and cut flowers for Mother's room.

I had known Louise since I was three years old, and I had always liked her. Her youngest daughter had been my first friend, and I had never forgotten an exciting visit to their house when they had a baby lamb that they fed with a bottle.

Pop wrote to his sister, not mentioning that he had visited Louise alone or that she had left her husband, "putting together what she's told me and what I've read in The Wall Street Journal and elsewhere, the family is worth, all together, somewhere between $30–$50 million dollars."

Some months after he had put Mother in the nursing home, Pop confided to me that he and Louise were in love. I believed him when he said he was in love, and I tried to understand his position. He had been tending his demented mother and his ailing wife. He was healthy and vigorous, and Mother's long illness was a strain on everyone.

I went to see her as often as I could, but I had little time off from my secretarial job, and I had to drive several hundred miles each way in the used Ford Falcon that Pop had helped me pick out, which required a can of oil each trip. I was afraid it would break down, and Sam and I would be stranded on the highway.

Every time Sam and I reentered the nursing home, my stomach knotted. Mother would be in her room, sleeping or watching television, or sometimes even doing a crossword puzzle. She scoffed at the activities offered — she swore she would never play bingo.

She was always friendly but didn't seem excited to see us. Sam was curious about the green plastic tubes in her nose, but a little frightened by her. She had never hugged or touched much; expressing affection seemed to make her uncomfortable. She had little to say, and talking made her short of breath. Sitting back in bed or in a wheelchair, her small breasts unbound and flattened downward, Mother gulped for air like a fish thrown on land.

Knowing that every good-bye might be our last, I tried each time I left her to prepare myself for never seeing her again. Then, upon every return, when I kissed her soft, wrinkled cheek, and breathed, beneath the odors of the nursing home, her sweet, familiar scent, I would wonder how I could have given her up.

I felt that Pop's involvement with Louise was a betrayal of Mother, but I was still immature enough, at twenty-seven, to adopt other people's opinions, and Pop wanted me to approve. Although he told me and my middle sister about Louise, he didn't tell my other brother or my oldest sister in Amsterdam.

Mother was very sick. She was going to die. Was Pop supposed to die with her? Louise, ten years younger, was healthy and energetic — a tall, handsome woman with an ample figure who, after her unhappy marriage, found Pop very charming.

If she answered many of Pop's needs, she answered many of mine, too. If he wanted a wife, I wanted a mother—one who was able to take an interest in my life. Mother had been sick since I was eighteen. When Sam was born, she hadn't come to be with me—she had already been ill for five years. And after spending Sam's second Christmas with us, she had caught such a bad cold that she had to go into the hospital.

On my first visit to Louise's house after Pop told me they were in love, she set out a little table for Sam, with a child-size chair and crayons and paper, and placed a vase of sweet-smelling yellow freesias in my bedroom. Struggling to raise Sam by myself, I longed for a mother's advice and comfort. But my own mother could not help me. She could not even help herself.

So if Pop was betraying Mother, wasn't I, too? I felt it would be ungenerous of me not to be glad that Pop had found love. I was impressed by the fact that such old people (sixty-five and fifty-five) could be in love.

It was just that Mother was still alive.

With Mother in the nursing home, Pop was free of her care. He was free, too, of housekeeping. Frank took care of all that, in addition to working at a men's clothing store.

Still, Pop didn't get his box business going. He got Mother declared mentally incompetent and got power of attorney to cash her dividend checks from Cornie's trust fund.

He would go stay with Louise at her Vermont house, and she would come to Plymouth to stay with him. They would visit Mother at the nursing home, drink a glass of sherry with her, then, leaving her there, go home together.

Mother continued to live in the nursing home—just a few miles from her house—for a full year. A few weeks before Thanksgiving of 1974, I received what would be my last letter from her. Her once-clear, strong handwriting was crabbed and shaky. Scribbled on a piece of torn-off white paper, it seemed like a note in a bottle from someone hoping for rescue, set adrift on the ocean that separated us.

Dearest,

*Thank you so much for nifty letters. And I even wrote
back, and I also wrote a note to your sister. She's
definitely coming for Thanksgiving and maybe before.
Is there any chance at all for you?*

*I can't wait to tell you some great stories of the
House of Nursing. One would think that it is a house
of gloom, or, at best, resignation, but this isn't entirely
true. Some of it is funny beyond belief, and some is
romantic, believe it or not. I'm going to tell you the
biography of my room-mate when next we meet. It's
too complicated to write about. Would you even think
that "tiny B" (which is what Pop named her) could
have a romantic life? Well, it strikes me that way,
even though it's a mighty queer brand of romanticism
(I don't mean "queer" that way).*

*Also, ask me to tell you a little biography of the
MIT professor across the hall. He's a touch romantic,
too. Well, lots of love to you all, and devotion and
romanticism, and all those there kissy things!*

I didn't really want to go "home" that Thanksgiving, to strap Sam into his car seat and drive all those miles into the sadness I always felt seeing Mother, but I went.

Louise and Frank were laughing together in the kitchen, which smelled of roasting turkey, fresh coffee, and cigarette smoke when Sam and I arrived at the back door. Pop's boxer, Nicky, bounded up and practically knocked Sam down, then wiggled around the kitchen, wagging his stubby tail, with Sam holding on to him.

"Hi, little sister!" Frank said in his constricted voice, dropping a light kiss on my cheek. Frank and I had only once had a personal conversation, when I had asked him how he could have left his wife and child. "It's easy," he had said. "You just walk away."

Now he waved and said hi to Sam, but he didn't touch him. Pop came into the kitchen from the living room, where he had been reading, and gave Sam an awkward embrace, saying, "Hello, little man!"

Louise, in a soft blue sweater, embraced me with a smile and hug, then bent down to kiss Sam in his bright yellow jacket and admire the tiny toy car he had kept in his hand during the trip. Sam's fine light-brown hair, released from its winter hat, stood straight up at his cowlick, as usual. He chattered to Louise about his car's many wonders.

As I carried my suitcase, hastily packed with our clothes for the weekend, through the dining room and living room, I saw that most of the piles of papers were gone. There were flowers on the dining room table and a different lamp by Mother's chair.

I went up the short staircase into what used to be my bedroom, a narrow space with a single bed, a dresser, and a tall bookcase with my Willa Cather books. The window, its blue-and-white curtains sewn by Mother, overlooked the winter-dried grape arbor across the front porch roof. Louise had set up a cot for Sam next to my bed. She had put a little vase of pink and white carnations and a clean white cloth on the dresser.

Down the hall in the small bathroom, I discovered new soft yellow towels, and inside the mirrored medicine cabinet, Louise's deodorant and toothbrush. Mother's old jar of Pond's face cream had been pushed to the side. I unscrewed the top and inhaled—its scent, like Aladdin's lamp, evoking Mother.

In the early evening, Pop brought Mother from the nursing home for the big meal. When he carried her in, it was as if the house darkened. A nurse had dressed her for the holiday in a synthetic paisley dress that kept slipping up as she lay on the couch, revealing her once-beautiful legs, mottled and shriveled, shod in bedroom slippers. Pale and waxen, she was too weak to sit up more than a few minutes. The children of some visiting friends looked curiously at her, silenced by her strangeness. She had forgotten whatever she had wanted to tell me about the romantic life of her roommate.

Before dinner, on my way to sit with her, I stopped by the dining table I had set with her celebratory white lace cloth, purple-and-pink china, and pearl-handled knives. From this spot, I could, for a moment, see into both kitchen and living room. In front of the fireplace, Mother, ashen-faced, the green tubes of her oxygen tank in her nose, lay crumpled on the stained rose velvet sofa, while in the fragrant kitchen, Pop swayed in an embrace with her old friend.

3

Smoke

We had set up a small table for the children. The adults crowded around the dining table, but I stayed for a few moments in the next room, near Mother, where she lay on the couch in front of the fire, her eyes closed.

Louise brought the steaming turkey to the table. I could smell its delicious warm aroma, and the scents, too, of the buttery mashed potatoes and creamed onions that Frank, wearing one of Mother's aprons, carried in and placed on the table, pushing the dog forcefully out of the way with his leg.

Chairs scraped, then Louise asked Pop to say grace. He read from the Anglican Book of Common Prayer, "O most merciful Father, we give thee humble thanks for this thy special bounty; beseeching thee to continue thy loving-kindness unto us," then added, "Good food, good meat, good God, let's eat!" to laughter, and the toast he always added for the dead, "And here's to those in the shade." I took Mother's cold hand in mine and turned her wedding ring, a thin, worn band of some inexpensive metal—all they could afford, she had told me, in the Depression—around on her finger.

"Mommy?" Sam called out, wondering where I was.

"Out here," I replied. He came to the doorway and looked at us. I held my free hand out to him. He crossed the room and leaned against me for a moment. He was warm and smelled like any healthy small child—a pure odor, like that of a new green plant. We kissed and he ran back into the dining room with the others. I heard him admonishing the dog, who had squeezed under the children's card table, begging for food.

Louise said, to follow up on the grace, "One of the beautiful miracles of this year has been that Frank and Pop have had each other. It's really fine when two people can fill each other's needs so simply and clearly."

Mother opened her eyes in the unseeing way people do when they're asleep, then closed them again. Louise was saying, "In my experience, every time I've left my life up to God, he's arranged it far better than I could ever have thought of."

Soon my middle sister came around the corner with a plate of food for Mother, and I returned to the dining room. Louise's turkey was good, but I preferred the plainer stuffing Mother used to make.

We had pumpkin pie with whipped cream, and coffee. Cigarettes were lit, and more wine poured. The small dining room was lively with voices and laughter. The children had gotten rowdy and were chasing one another through the kitchen and dining room when I got up to collect Sam for bed. Pop picked Mother up to carry her out to the car and back to the nursing home. Frank held the back door open for them, and everyone called out good night to her, though her eyes were still closed, and she didn't reply. I took Sam over to kiss her good night.

I was glad to be able to remain in the house, redolent with the smells of good food, but Mother was being returned to where it smelled of disinfectant.

Later, I crept into my darkened room upstairs, where Sam, in his favorite fire-truck pajamas, was asleep in the cot next to my bed, his toy car clasped in his fist, his mouth open, his lashes long and dark against his face. His breathing was easy and regular.

The next day, I left Sam with Louise while I went downtown to look in shops. When I came into the kitchen, pleased with my purchase of a new lipstick, Louise straightened up from fitting a cookie tray into the oven to say that the nursing home had just called. Mother's death was imminent.

Pop, Frank, my middle sister, and I piled into Pop's old gray Falcon to go be with her.

She wasn't conscious. Her roommate had been moved out temporarily, and we were left alone with her except for the occasional, quiet visits of a nurse checking her vital signs. The beige window curtains had been drawn; a few notes from us, a few photos, were tacked on her bulletin board. Her eyeglasses were folded, unneeded, on her bedside table.

I saw that dying, like childbirth, required labor. I sat close to Mother's head, wiping the perspiration from her face. I wiped the spittle from her mouth, turning my head to avoid the rotten-sweet smell of the exhalations from her ruined lungs.

We sat with her for about six hours. At some point, because I had read that people who are unconscious may still be able to hear, I sang several of her favorite hymns, hymns whose solemnity, mystery, and beauty, whose strange, even frightening, images and eerily complex syntax had always made the hair rise on my arms:

> Let all mortal flesh keep silence, and with fear and
>   trembling stand,
> Ponder nothing earthly minded, for with blessing in
>   his hand,
> Christ Our God to earth descendeth, our full homage
>   to demand.

And:

> Now my tongue, the mystery telling
> Of the glorious Body sing
> And the Blood, all price excelling
> Which the Gentiles' Lord and King
> Once on earth among us dwelling
> Shed for this world's ransoming.

Although Mother appeared to be unconscious in those last hours, there was a startling moment when she unexpectedly opened her eyes, gazed at us with a look of puzzlement, and murmured, "Are you all still here?" Pop moved close to her, calling her by her childhood nickname, "Tidie?"

After that, her life force steadily lessened, like a fire burned down to coals at the end of the evening. Her body, except for her head, got cooler and cooler. Her breaths came more slowly, with longer and longer pauses between them. As I waited to see if she would draw another, I held my own breath. I felt that I might scream—imagined that if I let go of my breath I would fly across the room like a released balloon. Finally, after the longest pause of all, and a last inhalation, her breathing simply stopped.

It was as if she had become smoke and had risen up the chimney of her body and out, to vanish into the dark sky.

Mother and her cigarette, 1972

4

Heirs

Leaving the larger upholstered chair for Pop, my sister and I each sat on one of the plain wooden chairs in the small office of the Beaman Funeral Home on Middle Street in Plymouth, not far from the library where Mother had so often taken out her stacks of mystery novels.

The Beaman Funeral Home was a family operation—since 1895, according to a small sign on a polished wooden side table—and Miss Anne Beaman, a middle-aged lady with a clean and dry appearance, a grave but not unpleasant look on her face, sat at the small desk across from Pop.

I had picked up one of the aqua-and-white pamphlets on the side table, titled "What Everyone Should Know," and had glanced through its pages about estate planning, death certificates, and Social Security.

For some reason, there was a drawing of the Jefferson Memorial on the first page, and at the bottom of each subsequent page, a different quotation from Jefferson, such as "the will of the people is the only legitimate foundation of any government." Miss Beaman must have thought Jefferson appropriate for a funeral home in historic Plymouth, known as "America's Home Town."

The pamphlet reminded me of another, "You're a Young Lady Now," which Mother had given me with my first package of Kotex sanitary napkins. The cover, pink and blue, featured a pigtailed girl in pants looking into a full-length mirror at an image of herself transformed into a sophisticated young lady wearing a dress. The cover was sprinkled with stardust.

Each pamphlet introduced me to a new world—menstruation and death. Each tried to euphemize the messy reality of the body's natural processes. The Kotex pamphlet emphasized being "dainty" and "fresh"—the funeral pamphlet addressed only the clean paper documents surrounding death.

Miss Anne Beaman told us, "I have her out back where it's cool." Mother's body was to be cremated, because it was cheaper than burial. Having lived through the Depression, Mother was what she had called "tight as a tick," and in addition, she had spoken with disgust of the financial exploitation she had read about in Jessica Mitford's book, *American Way of Death*. We picked out the simplest, least expensive coffin in Miss Beaman's small showroom of glossy coffins, and certainly one without a white satin pillow and lining.

Once the ashes were returned, there would be a graveside service, presided over by the priest from Mother's Catholic church.

A few days after that service, Pop wrote to my oldest sister, who had been unable to come from Amsterdam:

> *Your mother's body went to Boston for cremation on Saturday and we buried the ashes in the plot where my brother and mother are on Monday morning with 12–15 people there. Thanks for the flowers, which were a rich and handsome sight. We put a few on the grave and took the rest home.*
>
> *As to your mother's death and me, I have known for a long time that her life would be short. Death will come to all of us, dear, and the sooner we come to a rational acceptance of that, the better we'll be able to handle deaths and the idea of death. In your mother's case, as in many others, the circumstances eventually come to a point where everyone (except, perhaps, the sick person) welcomes death as the best of several things which*

might happen. It would have been very difficult for
me to have your mother lying as a vegetable with a
heart still beating, and the expense was intolerable.
I have almost exactly the amount of cash on hand to
pay the last two months at the nursing home, drug
bills, the hairdresser, the funeral director, etc. and that's
all the cash I have.

Pop wrote that it was the expense of keeping Mother alive that was "intolerable"—not her suffering, her years of illness, the possibility that she might have been "lying as a vegetable with a heart still beating." He decided this was a good time to finally tell my oldest sister about Louise:

I am grateful that you want me to find someone
else whom I love and who loves me and I am grateful
beyond words that I have found one. Louise and I
have grown into a wonderful relationship and will
live together, sans marriage because of her alimony,
which stops if she marries. We have had heart-warming
approval and approbation from all our children; you are
the last to know.

Mother's estate took about six months to be settled. Pop was not going to inherit her trust fund, because Cornie had specifically set it up to pass on to us children. But Pop told us it was rightfully his—if only Cornie had liked him—so he would expect us to turn our shares over to him.

My oldest sister was furious at him and refused. Pop responded that he would disown her. My sister's reaction made me wonder for the first time why Pop hadn't managed money better. I had never thought about it, and I was used to doing what he wanted. And shouldn't the money really have gone to him? At first, I didn't dare cross him—he could disown me, too. But as it turned out, my middle sister and I gave him the interest from our shares for a time but kept the principal.

Pop was selling the house and moving to California to live with Louise in her new house overlooking the Pacific. Frank continued to live in Mother's old room and work at the men's clothing store while he waited for his inheritance. He repainted the downstairs of the house a jarring bright blue.

On one of my infrequent visits to Plymouth before the estate was settled, Frank surprised me with the gift of a pearl necklace in a white satin-lined leather case. He had a whole box of them—some new business idea. "For my baby sister" he said, laughing. I assumed the pearls were imitation but discovered, years later, that they were real.

After the inheritances were finally distributed, to everyone's surprise, Frank got married again. I never met this fourth wife, but Louise told me they had bought a fancy car and a new house.

Then, one evening soon after they had moved in, Frank left his wife a note: "I won't be home tonight, or ever." He disappeared, and we never heard from him again.

5

A Late-Night Thought

Five more presidents had been elected since Mother's nemesis, Nixon, had resigned in disgrace and Frank had disappeared.

I was lying in bed one night, nearly asleep, when the hair suddenly rose on my arms. I sat straight up. I had had a thought that had never before occurred to me: maybe Mother had been right when she claimed that Frank had tried to kill her.

I had not looked back at Mother's death or that awful last year of her life. Witnessing her decline had been like watching her lower herself into boiling oil.

When she died, I had been twenty-eight, divorced, and a single parent. My own life and my own problems had occupied the twenty-two years that had passed since then. Pop had died, ten years after Mother. I had seldom even thought about Frank.

I had remarried, had another child, divorced, and married Reg. I had earned my master's degree in social work, spent a decade working as a therapist, and written several books for children. Sam had grown up and was on his own, and my daughter, Kate Elizabeth—her middle name in honor of Mother—was at home for her last year before leaving for college.

I was fifty, and for the first time I had the opportunity to slow down, to think about all that had happened in the past. I bought a used four-drawer file cabinet and organized Mother and Pop's letters and all the family papers that had been passed on to me. I made a file for each year of my life.

As I thought about Mother's accusation all those years ago, I realized that, if I could read her medical records, I might be able to learn why she had been considered paranoid and, perhaps, put to rest the disturbing idea that Frank had tried to harm her. As a clinical social worker, I had been trained to assess patients' mental states and was used to reading medical charts.

It didn't seem likely that I could still get Mother's records, but I figured I might as well try, and sent a request to the hospital in Plymouth.

After several weeks, when I had gotten no response, I telephoned. A woman with a notable Massachusetts accent told me, "We've been working on your mother's records this week," adding, "I know that you're her daughter and all, but there's sensitive information, and we need you to sign a form before we can send you the records, OK?"

"Sensitive?" I knew that term was used to denote drug and alcohol abuse or psychiatric information, and for a moment, I wondered if Mother had told the hospital staff some deeply hidden secret. Had she attempted suicide? Had Pop been physically abusive to her? Then I wondered why I chose those sorts of possible "secrets" and not others.

What did I really know about my own family?

I returned the form and waited impatiently for the records to arrive. Finally, after ten days, a large manila envelope arrived in our black metal mailbox. I tore it open to find an inch-and-a-half-thick stack of photocopies of typewritten and handwritten records. Sinking down into the old red wing chair I had inherited from Mother, the chair in which she had so often read, I began looking over her records.

Variously titled "Personal History," "Summary Sheet," "Physical Examination," "Operative Record," "Consultation Record," "Discharge Summary," and "Outpatient Department," they were in chronological order, beginning with Mother's first admission to the hospital in 1965 and ending only a few weeks prior to her death in 1974.

The typists who had transcribed the records had made a number of obvious errors, the most startling one a description of Mother's genitals as "normal male" instead of "normal female."

That certainly would have been "sensitive information." But Mother had borne five children, and I had seen her naked—she was definitely female.

In the earliest record, Mother, at fifty-six, had been described as "a well-nourished and well-developed white female about the stated age" but only five years later as "an elderly white female who appears older than her stated age, with evidence of weight loss and chronic illness."

The initial records included energetic plans for her treatment. But by the time she was sent to the nursing home, the doctor had written, "The prognosis is extremely grave. No potential for rehabilitation."

I sat for a while, silent and sad.

Then I continued reading, and came upon the report written after Pop had taken her to the emergency room:

> This is a 62-year-old white female who has had a long history of chronic lung disease, dependency on oxygen at home. The past ten days she's had increasing episodes of mental confusion. First of all when she was out of touch with reality, secondly when she would appear to be confused as to time, place, and person. 3. When she had been hallucinating, seeing people around her that were not there and also having delusions that her son or her husband were trying to kill her. In particular she has accused her son of trying to "do her in."
>
> She has also yesterday morning had an episode in which she spent about 15 minutes dipping her eyeglasses in a glass of milk, lifting them up, deliberately lapping them off and putting them back in again and repeating this episode. Tonight she refused to take medications from her family at home and stated that she wouldn't do anything that they asked her to do and stated that she was afraid they were going to kill her. She was finally brought into the hospital for further evaluation as to consultation with the psychiatrist. For details of her past history see the old record.

Mother's use of the phrase "do her in" reminded me of all those mystery novels she had liked to read.

I went upstairs and rummaged through my file cabinet. I located the letter Pop had written me about taking her to the emergency room:

> Frank, your mother and I went to your sister's for a
> weekend on October 18th. We had oxygen troubles
> going up and your mother got upset. She was already
> quite weak and we made a bed-like thing for her in
> the backseat of the wagon and had the rear part full
> of oxygen tanks and our bag. She spent all the time
> at your sister's in bed and by the time we got home
> on the twenty-first she seemed exhausted.
>
> Soon after we got back, we began to notice little
> paranoidal spells and confusion. We took her medicines
> away from her and now Frank gives her the daily ration
> in a little vial each morning and we have a check table
> where we note when she takes what.
>
> She woke Frank and me up at 12:30 to tell me that
> he was trying to kill us both. She is normal this morning
> but we have had one of these little spells about once a
> day for ten days. She sort of drifts into them and then
> drifts out after a while, sometimes not remembering
> she's had them. They have been frequent enough so
> that I think this is going to be a continuing thing to
> cope with. The next problem is that we can't cope with
> it for very long at home. I've just told the doctor about
> last night's episode. He is going to call a geriatric
> psychiatrist whom I had to see my mother a couple
> of times. He says he has a hunch there might be an
> organically created psychosis because of using steroids
> over a long time.
>
> So that's the story at the moment, not a happy one
> but there are resources to deal with it. Frank is being
> wonderful and absolutely indispensable.

Pop had written that "she woke Frank and me up at 12:30 to tell me that he was trying to kill us both." But the hospital reported that Mother had been "having delusions that her son or her husband were trying to kill her."

Why had Pop asked Frank to dispense her medicines, and not done it himself? Why had he used the expression "a little vial" of medicine? "A little vial" sounded like something else out of one of Mother's mystery novels.

I visualized the arrangement of the rooms of the Plymouth cottage. How could Mother have managed, tethered to her oxygen tanks on the first floor, to wake Pop up, past midnight, in his second-floor bedroom, to tell him of her fear? She must have been really afraid if she had disconnected herself from her oxygen, walked through the kitchen, through the dining room, and through the living room, to reach the bottom of the stairs and call out.

Did she even have the breath to call out? Had she, instead, stayed in her room and rung a bell? How could Pop have heard that? Wanting only to wake Pop, to seek his protection, she must have unavoidably awakened Frank, too, since the small upstairs bedrooms were very close to one another and to the staircase.

I had not known that Mother was disoriented about time and place, or that she had hallucinated, or what, exactly, she had hallucinated. The hospital staff had not directly observed her disorientation or hallucinations—they were just reporting what Pop had told them.

Had he told me, too, and had I forgotten? Or had he never told me about it at all? It was clear that Mother's behavior had been bizarre—dipping her eyeglasses in milk and lapping it off!

I put the records down on my lap. What reason would Frank have had to kill her? Of course, he knew that when she died he would inherit his share of Cornie's trust fund—$35,000. But Mother was obviously not going to live very long, anyway. Had he decided he couldn't wait?

When would Frank have had the opportunity to kill her? Pop was there. But Pop had left Mother in Frank's care when he took that first trip to see Louise, and he had taken other trips, as well. He often left the house to do errands. So Frank had been alone with Mother many times.

What could Frank have done to her? Pop had written about

how anxious Mother was about her oxygen. She couldn't turn the valves herself—Frank or Pop had to do it. What if Frank had simply turned off her oxygen? What if he had given her the wrong pills?

Was it just a coincidence that she had seemed all right before Frank moved in? Even though he had lied repeatedly, deserted his first wife and child, married unsuspecting women and stolen their money, embezzled from an employer who trusted him—even though he was capable of being charming and sweet as he was deceiving people—that didn't prove he was capable of attempted murder. To kill his own mother—he would have to be heartless.

But hadn't we seen that he was heartless?

Pop had written me that Frank was being "absolutely indispensable." Now, I wondered, indispensable for what?

Mother had been in the care of a nice doctor with whom she and Pop were friends. She had worked as his medical secretary before she got sick. He would surely have noticed if anything was amiss. I decided to try to find him.

6

Paranoia

The nursing home was still in the phone book, and when I called, it turned out that the director was the son of Mother's doctor. That made sense, because her doctor had been one of the owners of the home.

When the director heard my name, he was very friendly—we had gone to the same high school, and our parents had been friends. He told me that his father had retired but still lived nearby. Unfortunately, the nursing home no longer had any of Mother's records, but he had his father's medical practice records stored in the basement. He would look to see if Mother's were among them, and if they were, he would ask his father if I could talk to him.

A few days later, after he had called back to say he had found them and given me his father's number, I sat down at Mother's old walnut desk and spread out the records I had already received from the hospital. I kept a framed photograph of Mother on her old desk. I liked to remember her that way, one leg tucked up beneath her in the red wing chair, a stack of books on the table next to her.

I dialed her doctor's number.

He greeted me cheerfully, "I really liked your mother and father! They were great people." I remembered him as a decent, tall, shambling man with a cowlick and an air of being perpetually overworked.

I told him that I had already gotten and read all of Mother's hospital records and that I was a clinical social worker. I said that I had been thinking recently about Mother's "paranoia," and I wondered what he might remember about her accusation against Frank. After a surprised pause, he said that he had Mother's records open on the desk in front of him, and he read to me the report by the hospital emergency room staff.

I listened politely, although I was familiar with the report, and then asked him if he remembered any further details. He didn't. He said he had no memory of the whole incident except what had been written down—understandable in a busy professional life, and with the events being from so long ago.

He pointed out that a psychiatrist had seen Mother several times, and he read me that doctor's report:

> This 62-year-old married female was admitted on 11-1-73 because of chronic lung disease, oxygen addiction, progressive weight loss, weakness, and mental confusion of ten days duration. She exhibited disorientation, visual hallucinations (people), paranoid delusions, and bizarre behavior. She has been on steroids.
>
> The patient was seen in bed while receiving nasal oxygen. She was friendly and went through the appropriate amenities. She understood I was a psychiatrist and told of her mother-in-law dominating the household and her resentment, mother-in-law going to a nursing home where she died two years ago. She expressed guilt over this. That was as far as she could pursue the subject. At my suggestion she told me of her happy marriage and spoke of each of her children. She mentioned their problems in a philosophical vein. When she again stopped, I asked about her emphysema. As she told me of this she was self-deprecating. And suddenly became confused, stated she had gotten her "time frame" mixed up, asked if she hadn't told me all of this before, and looked at me as if I were someone else. "I know it's rude but could we continue this later?" I agreed.

Also during the brief interview she asked for the tissue box but had to gesture as if she could not find the proper name. But she did repeat my name. She did not offer any paranoid material nor did she appear to hallucinate. Her mood was generally sad. Her affect was appropriate and moderated well.

With the mildly abnormal (diffusely so) EEG [electroencephalogram, a brain-wave recording], history, and interview I would conclude that this patient suffers from an acute and/or chronic brain syndrome of unknown etiology [cause]. Hypoxia [not enough oxygen] could certainly give such a picture and steroids could too. The latter usually, in my experience, lead to a more florid [elaborate] picture with a lot of primary process like associations (i.e. thought disorder). In a woman of 62 Alzheimer's Dementia is a possibility but sudden onset does not favor it. A vascular accident [a stroke] would explain the sudden onset but not the lack of lateralizing signs.

The plan of decreasing the steroids, the use of Tranxene and Thorazine [a tranquilizer and an antipsychotic], and, if she quiets, placement in a nursing home seem appropriate. I don't feel the problem is basically emotional; a neurological opinion might be helpful.

I listened quietly, although I had already read this report, too — it was on the desk in front of me. I told him that while I understood his and the psychiatrist's thinking about Mother's condition, I was wondering, since he had been friends with my parents, if they had ever told him about Frank, and I summarized Frank's troubled history. He didn't make any response to what I told him — simply said he hadn't known any of it, had thought that Frank had come home to help my parents out. Probably he didn't know what to say, or perhaps he was afraid of being held responsible for not having taken Mother's accusation seriously. I realized that neither he nor the psychiatrist would have had any reason to think Mother's accusation could have been true.

He offered to send me copies of his records. Thanking him, I asked if he would mind sending the originals so I could copy them myself and send them back. I told him that I wanted to be sure I had seen everything that was in her record; there might be something I would consider important that he had not thought to mention. He readily agreed. I had the feeling he might think *I* was being paranoid. I wondered, just a little, if I was.

7

Finding Out

During that last year of Mother's life, one nurse had been very important to her—a middle-aged woman whom Mother had referred to as "my dearie." Maybe if I could talk to her, she would remember something that could help me.

I called the nursing home director again. He thought at once of a Mrs. Egan who had been one of their most valued and longest-serving employees. She had retired, but he had stayed in touch with her and would ask if she would be willing to talk with me. He soon called me back with her number.

I sat down with a notepad and pencil at Mother's Iowa grandmother's walnut desk, noticing, as usual, the burn mark on it where Mother had laid down a cigarette. I had been rereading a note she had written to me that last year:

Darling—

Your loverley little note was dated October 4 but I received it just about an hour ago. Is that the fault of the House or the U.S. Postal Service—neither of which is a lot dependabler than the other?

Anyhow—thank you for the darling note—and for all the others in the past. From now on I'm going to try to reply, even if it's only a few words—because I think of you all so much & I might even just write you a sentence

of conversation. Don't feel pushed about doing it
but once in a while put a couple of words on a card
too please. Much much love to you and hugs and
love to Sammy too.

She had drawn three hearts after her name.

I dialed Mrs. Egan's number. She would be in her eighties. It had been more than two decades since she had cared for Mother. She probably wouldn't remember her.

"Hello?" said a soft, elderly voice.

I introduced myself, reminded her of Mother's name, and thanked her for her kindness all those years ago. "You were a kind of angel to her," I said.

"Well, thank *you*," she said. "I appreciate that, because right now I'm feeling a little low myself." She explained that she was at a crossroads, having to decide whether she needed to give up her apartment and live with her daughter.

"I've been trying to remember," she said. "Was your mother alone in her room or did she have a roommate?"

"She had a roommate," I replied.

"I'm trying to figure . . . looking from the nurse's station was she to the right or was she to the left?" she asked.

"I wish I could remember," I replied, "but I'm not sure."

How to describe Mother to her? I said, "She was a very intelligent, very likable woman. At the time she came into the nursing home, she had supposedly become paranoid. She had been on oxygen for about a year."

"I'm thinking, I'm thinking . . . I think I remember," she said. There was silence. Then she said, "Now!" and it was as if her memory of Mother suddenly bloomed. "She was by the window. And her roommate's name was Mrs. Brown."

"Yes!" I said, remembering Mother writing me about "tiny B."

"Yes, that was it," said Mrs. Egan. "Now I remember her. And I do remember she had times when she was very depressed."

"I would think so," I replied. "At the time, my oldest brother, Frank, was living with my parents. And Mother became afraid that he was trying to kill her. Do you remember her ever talking about that?"

"Well . . ." Mrs. Egan said, "I know she had some feelings about *somebody* in that house where you used to live."

"Did she express some of her fears to you?"

"Yes, I think she did."

"What did she tell you?"

"That her husband was not faithful."

"Oh!" I exclaimed. So Mother had known. I felt as if I had been struck by a stone that had been falling toward me all these years.

"But that was true!" I cried. "That wasn't paranoid! That was true!"

"I think that's what bothered her more than anything else," said Mrs. Egan.

I could not speak for a moment. Then I said, "My father and my mother's old friend—you probably met her, because she went with my father to see Mother at the nursing home—began having an affair. But they thought Mother was not aware of what was happening."

"That's the impression I got," said Mrs. Egan.

"But it was so cruel of them, I think, looking back!" I said.

"Yes, it was," she agreed. "But they in their own way were consoling each other, and I think they were probably more concerned with each other than they were with her, because they maybe thought there was no hope for her to improve."

Remembering that sentence from Mother's medical record, "There is no potential for rehabilitation," I said, "There wasn't any hope for her to improve."

"No," said Mrs. Egan.

Then she added, "I do remember her now. She was such a beautiful woman in so many ways."

"Anything you can tell me would be valuable to me," I said.

"I can remember one night, we must have had some sort of religious talk, and she said, 'I'm at peace now because there was a figure that came and spoke to me and said, "Don't be afraid."'"

"And did you think that was a genuine experience?"

"I supposed so." She was silent a moment. "That's about it," Mrs. Egan said.

It seemed time to end the conversation. I thanked her once more, and as I was about to hang up, she said, "Only . . ."

I waited.

"Your mother always wanted to go back home. She didn't understand why she couldn't go back to her home."

8

Records of the Deceased

As he had promised, Mother's doctor sent me her records. They were in a worn manila folder, the word *deceased* written next to her name on the outside.

Most of them were duplicates of the ones I had already gotten from the hospital, but there were a few new items. There was a letter from Mother's previous doctor in Cincinnati, summarizing her medical history from 1952 until 1962, when she and Pop and I had moved to Plymouth. He had written, "I not only admire Elizabeth immensely, but she also worked for me for some years and I consider her a good friend. I hope you have the pleasure caring for her that I have had all these years. Give her my love."

This seemed a very personal comment to include in a medical summary, but Mother and Pop had always gone to doctors who were also friends, which, when I thought about it now, didn't seem to be a good thing to do. In the Cincinnati doctor's summary, he hadn't included Mother's longtime use of the tranquilizer Miltown or her hospitalization for what Pop told us was a "rest" after Frank left his first wife and child—which I clearly remembered because Mother had been in the hospital on my birthday.

There was a letter from Pop, addressed to the Plymouth doctor at his home and not his office, in which Pop claimed that his work was being "seriously affected" by having to take care of Mother.

There was a letter from the nursing home, dated two months after Mother's placement, stating that she no longer needed "skilled care." But instead of taking her home, Pop had moved her to the new nursing home owned by their doctor.

There was a final report from the psychiatrist, written only weeks before Mother died:

> Prepared for my coming, the patient indeed recognized me on sight and welcomed me by name. Alert, attentive, and oriented, her speech was logical and coherent. Occasionally she would have trouble with a word or a name. Neither delusions nor hallucinations were elicited. Her affect was appropriate and affective. Her mood was somewhat depressed.
>
> Staff reveal that she is more agitated in the late afternoon and evening. At times she is forgetful and confused, but she has not hallucinated since late spring. Her Thorazine appears to help. Around her oxygen she requires considerable reassurance and attention. Staff appear quite knowledgeable about her care; an up-to-date and complete nursing care plan is available. Her psychotropic medication is appropriate. She participates in some activities. I doubt that more or different care is indicated at this time.
>
> Diagnosis: Chronic brain syndrome with probable chronic hypoxia. Depression, mild. Emphysema.

The psychiatrist had added a note: "Mr. Spelman really is quite full of guilt about her being there, but he needn't be."

And there was one final item—Mother's electrocardiogram, a visual record of the activity of her heart. Those sharp black spikes on white paper made a picture of the sound I must have heard in her womb.

9

A Second Opinion

I met informally with a geriatric psychiatrist I knew. Maria was a woman about my own age with an intelligent, curious face. In the past, we had shared the care of several patients, and I respected her. She met me for coffee in the large, brightly lit, echoing cafeteria of the teaching hospital that employed her.

I had brought with me Mother's psychiatric reports, a list of all her medications, and her EEG—the recording of her brain's electrical activity.

Maria drank her coffee and listened attentively while I described Frank's history. When I was finished, she told me that Frank reminded her of a patient she had once had; a very attractive, charming young man. He had completely won her trust, and she had been certain that he could not have committed some awful deed of which he had been accused. She had been stunned when she learned that he had. He had seemed so sincere, so trustworthy, and so likable.

I handed Mother's records to her, stirring my coffee in its Styrofoam cup as she looked them over. The hospital cafeteria was noisy; groups of health-care workers clad in green surgical scrubs, paper booties, and caps laughed loudly at a table near ours.

After looking over the records, Maria commented that the diagnosis of chronic brain syndrome was essentially meaningless

—a general term indicating there was no way to be certain about what was causing the problem.

She said that Mother's EEG was definitely abnormal. But in the absence of more information, there was no way to interpret what it meant.

Maria did not think that the dose of steroids Mother had been taking was the cause of her behavior. Nor, in her opinion, was lack of oxygen. She thought it was possible that a sudden withdrawal from tranquilizers, such as the Miltown that Mother had taken for many years, could have caused delirium tremens–like hallucinations.

Regarding Mother's bizarre action of dipping her eyeglasses in her milk, Maria said that such behavior could indicate late-onset schizophrenia, but there had been nothing in Mother's prior life to support that diagnosis.

Shaking her head a little, she concluded that it was impossible to be clear about what had happened. Frank's behavior and history—and Pop's—made her think that "there was more than meets the eye." It seemed possible that Frank might have tried to kill Mother, but on the other hand, Mother could have been paranoid for reasons we did not know. Only an autopsy could really have told us. It was decades too late for that.

I found the phone number of Mother's psychiatrist, who had written that final report.

I called and left a message saying who I was and what I wanted to talk to him about. My call was not returned.

When I called again, a crabby, guarded-sounding elderly man answered. I told him that I was sorry to bother him, but—afraid he would hang up on me—I reminded him that my uncle had been his colleague, and added that I was a licensed mental health professional.

He paused a moment, then said, "I have no records of any patients."

"I have your records in front of me," I said. "I have all of Mother's records from the hospital and I already talked with her doctor, who also sent me all of his records."

He was silent a moment.

"I'm retired," he said.

"I know you are. And I *am* sorry to bother you, but since I do have these records you wrote, I thought maybe you could help me understand what happened."

"Well . . ." he replied, and he didn't hang up.

He asked me to remind him where he had seen Mother, how many times, and what the situation was. I told him, quoting from his reports.

Then I told him about Frank. He said, "It's impossible to tell. Even if we had known about your brother—she had a chronic brain syndrome—an organic brain syndrome . . . a person, especially an elderly person, can become very paranoid as a result of various medications, very easily."

"Oh?" I replied.

"Have you ever had major surgery?" he asked. He was about to undergo his third surgery for a hip replacement. "You can get very paranoid during your recovery," he said.

"I see," I replied. "What do you think about the possibility that Mother might have had a reaction to withdrawing from tranquilizers?

"Ah!" he replied, "That is where I do not go. I have a rule: never try to reconstruct, because you can be very wrong."

I thanked him again for talking with me and hung up.

I would never know exactly what had happened.

10

Finding Frank

There had been only one bubble on the surface of the pond into which Frank had vanished. A few years after Mother died, my middle sister got a phone call from a man in California who was looking for Frank. Unbeknownst to my sister, Frank had given her name as a reference on a mortgage application he had cosigned with this man. He had subsequently disappeared, riding off on the man's motorcycle.

When Pop had died, ten years after Mother, he had left a few thousand dollars to each of us, but Frank had not appeared to claim his money. None of us had looked for him.

I wanted to find out what had happened to him, but I did not want to talk to him. I did not want him to know I had looked for him. I just wanted to know where he was.

The development of the Internet had made it possible to search for him without having to hire a private detective. Because I had his Social Security number—Pop had saved his application for it—I was able to go online to the Social Security Death Index.

After nearly a quarter century of wondering what had happened to Frank, it took only a moment to find out. He had died two years earlier. When I saw his name, date of death, and Social Security number on the computer screen, my head jerked backward as if I'd accidentally walked into a glass door.

When I called Social Security, I was told they couldn't give me any further information.

Since the only clue to Frank's whereabouts had come from that man who had called from California, I wrote to the California Office of Vital Records to request a death certificate. But a few weeks later, when I received an official envelope from the state, I opened it to find a "certification of no record":

> This is to certify that an examination has been made of the Statewide Index in the Office of State Registrar of Vital Statistics covering the event shown and no reference to this event was found therein.

That left forty-nine states I would have to search. I needed to come up with a better way.

The Social Security office I chose to visit was clean but drab, carpeted with brown speckled institutional carpeting and furnished with about ten hard plastic chairs. A few half-dead plants drooped from white plastic pots. A tired-looking armed security guard sat on a stool inside the door.

I took a number, as instructed by a sign, and sat down to wait.

The clerk, a woman of middle age, sat behind a scuffed Plexiglas service window. She peered up irritably through the reading glasses she had looped around her neck with a purple cord. The peeved tone in her voice as she dealt with the people ahead of me was discouraging—I wouldn't be able to find out anything here. I flipped through an old, worn-out copy of *Car and Driver* magazine. The first car of our family's that I remembered had been a shiny, rounded Morris Minor; Frank, a new driver, had crushed the bumper, and Pop had been furious.

Finally, my number was called. "Can I help you?" the clerk asked, in a tone of voice that implied she would rather do anything but. Smiling at her, I lowered my voice so that the others waiting there couldn't hear me. "Oh, I hope so. I just found out on the Social Security Death Index that my brother, who was gone from our family for many years, has died."

"Oh?" she replied, against her will, it seemed, half interested.

"We've been looking for him for a long time. And the thing is, the index gave me the date of his death but it didn't say where, or whether or not he has any survivors. And my family would really like to know, if we could, where he died, so that we could know what happened, and put all this to rest."

A computer terminal was to the right of the clerk's chair, with several school photos of a young girl taped to it—her granddaughter, I imagined.

"We can't tell you that," she said tartly. But I sensed that she might feel sorry for me. She looked like a woman who had known her share of troubles.

"Oh. I understand." I said. "It's just that . . . it would mean so much to my mother to be able to find out where her son was buried."

I handed the clerk the piece of paper with Frank's Social Security number. She glanced around and lowered her own voice. "Do you have a pencil?" she asked. "Write this down."

She clicked the computer keys, then told me, very softly, that Frank had last worked in San Diego in 1993, and that his disability payments had been sent to his home address in Tijuana, Mexico.

"Thank you, my mother will never forget that you did this for her," I whispered.

I left the office in disbelief. Tijuana, Mexico?

Suddenly, I didn't believe that Frank was dead. He had been up to his old tricks. He had probably faked his death to get insurance or to get away from someone. I had heard you could buy anything you wanted in Tijuana, including a death certificate. Tijuana!

But the staff of the American consulate there obtained his death certificate for me. They put me in touch with the hospital—in the richest neighborhood of the city—where I learned he had died, after thirteen days, of lung and heart disease.

A phone call to his home number was answered by a woman who said she was the maid. She told me that Frank had rented a room in the house, which had been owned by a woman friend, for the past ten years. He had been sick with "problems in his lungs." His woman friend had since died, too. Frank had left no family.

Some weeks later, I received Frank's Mexican death certificate. On heavy ivory paper, stamped with the official seal of the Registro Civil of Tijuana, and listed under "Datos del Finado" (facts of the dead or "ended" person) were Frank's correct place and date of birth. Everything seemed to be in order.

I felt no affection for Frank. But because he had been Mother's child, I placed his baby photograph on my kitchen "altar"—a shelf above the table where I kept a small wooden Buddha statue that Reg had given me, a candle, and flowers. The Buddha's serene face and posture and the calm, smooth lines of his robe seemed to promise hope of some larger perspective from which all events, no matter how painful, might be viewed with understanding and acceptance, might even contain the seed of some unforeseeable future good.

I lit a candle for Frank. He had been a beautiful boy, with light, curly hair, Mother's eyes, and endearing large ears.

I had checked our black metal mailbox eagerly every day for six weeks, waiting for an envelope from the Freedom of Information Office in the Social Security Administration, but then, after all, I missed its arrival. I came downstairs one afternoon to find a rigid brown cardboard mailer marked, in capital letters, PRIORITY, addressed to me, lying on the piano bench. A friend who was staying with us had brought it in.

I opened it to find, after a cover letter from the Freedom of Information officer, Frank's disability file—a half-inch-thick pile of white papers, bound together through punched holes with red satin ribbon, and sealed with an eagle-embossed gold foil sticker. It looked like the second-place winner of a grade-school contest.

I glanced at the letter—it explained that the names of Frank's wives had been deleted from the record—and carefully turned to the first page of the disability file, a photocopy of Frank's birth

En atención a su solicitud de fecha   anterior me permito Adjuntar a Usted, tres

Certificado de **DEFUNCIONES** de nombre de **C.**   que se

sirviera requerir a esta Oficialía del Registro Civil a mi cargo.

Sin otro particular por el momento, me despido cordialmente.

A T E N T A M E N T E
SUFRAGIO EFECTIVO, NO REELECCION.
EL C. OFICIAL 01 DEL REGISTRO CIVIL

LIC. MANUEL QUIQUIN GONZALEZ.

FAVOR DE TOMAR NOTA DE COSTOS POR DERECHOS:
BUSQUEDA DE DATOS CUANDO NO MANDAN COPIA DE ACTA: ----42.00
COPIAS CERTIFICADAS DE ACTAS--------------------------------------65.00
INEXISTENCIA (incluye derechos p/ búsqueda x 5 años):-------------85.00

MOG/mls.

A portion of Frank's official death notice from Tijuana

certificate. In an odd coincidence, it had been filed on the same day that, sixty-two years later, he had died.

When I turned the next page, I gasped. It was a very bad photocopy of Frank's passport picture—his face looked like it had been burned to a crisp. Only his eyes shone out whitely, but I was sure it was him—I recognized his ears.

The staff person who had interviewed Frank when he had applied for disability had described him as "pleasant and articulate." Frank had signed his name to his application, attesting that "all the information I have given is true," but he had lied about a few unimportant things, just as my oldest sister said he had done long ago, stating that his "two brothers" were in good health, that he had been married three times (I knew of four), and that his father had "died of old age."

There were several medical reports from his Mexican doctor, translated into English. I read that Frank had suffered from emphysema—Mother's disease—caused by his "three packs of cigarettes a day for over thirty years." He had had a condition called cor pulmonale, in which the destruction of his lungs had damaged his heart.

Frank's arms and legs were swollen. Blood vessels in his mouth were broken. His skin was discolored—a color described, in translation, as "pink buff." The doctor had written, "The patient has the ability to stand only one hour, to remain seated two hours. The only thing he can do without difficulty is to crouch normally."

Frank had run away from everything. But, in the end, he had not been able to run away from himself.

Frank's photocopied passport picture

PART TWO

My Mother's Past

11

Sacred Lands

In 1854, eight years after Iowa became a state, Mother's great-grandparents settled in the valley of the river known by the Winnebago Indians as Wa-shood Ne-shun-a-ga-tah, later called the Cedar.

One interpretation of the name *Iowa* is "beautiful land." A history book described it as a "gently undulating prairie with narrow belts of timber along the streams." In those days, the waters of the Cedar "sparkled with black bass, rock bass, and silver bass; pickerel, muscalongue, wall-eye pike, red-horse, mud catfish, bullheads, chub, the dace, eels, and abundant minnows and shiners. There were buffalo, elk, deer, and black bears; wildcats and lynxes, large gray wolves and small prairie wolves; beavers, badgers, otters and muskrats." There was sometimes even still heard "the scream of the panther."

The Winnebago, who called themselves Hochungra, or "people of the big voices," sometimes returned from their exile in reservations to visit their homelands, and as they passed up and down the river in summer and fall, their custom was to place wisps of June grass on the graves of their dead.

One hundred forty-three years after my great-great-grandparents settled at the Cedar River, eighty-six years after Mother was born in Mason City, I traveled to Iowa in search of the past.

It was a chilly late-March day. In a deep green rental car that still smelled new, I drove away from the Mason City airport under a dark and overcast prairie sky. The radio announced that a spring snowstorm was on its way. My plane had gotten in just in time.

Checking in and leaving my small suitcase at a motel close to the old downtown, I found my way to the Mason City Public Library, an elegant 1939 building designed by the Chicago architectural firm Holabird and Root, set on a seven-acre lot full of trees.

Inside the library, in a glass case, I found a collection of Mason City High School yearbooks and looked through them for the year Mother graduated, 1927. I remembered her able to walk only haltingly, stopping every few steps to lean over so she could breathe. In her yearbook, I discovered with pleasure that she had won the school's highest athletic honor; she had been a swimming champion, basketball player, and president of the Girls' Athletic Association. Turning the pages, I came to Mother's senior photograph. Her eyes gazed confidently out at me from the face of a strong, cheerful, healthy young woman. I reluctantly put the yearbook back on the shelf.

Mother had never talked about her father Sam's death when she was a child, except to say that he had died of appendicitis. But she had kept a silver-framed photo of him in her bedroom, where no other photos were kept, not even of us children. After she died, I had found an engraved announcement of his death, on November 30, 1918, and an empty envelope from St. Luke's Hospital in Chicago, with Mother's childhood nickname, Tidie, written on it in Cornie's hand.

In that silver-framed photo, her father Sam is wearing a suit, tie, and gleaming leather dress shoes. He has a white handkerchief in his pocket, and a small white flower in his lapel. His overcoat is tucked over one arm, and he holds a small leather suitcase in the other hand.

In the background of the photo you can see a stone column, a roped-off flight of stairs, and a shadowy doorway with a sign. Under a magnifying glass, you can read the words *Clerk* and *Phone*. It could be a train station.

It is with sorrow we announce
the death of our Vice-President and Secretary
Samuel A. Schneider
on Saturday, the thirtieth of November
nineteen hundred and eighteen
Security National Bank
Mason City Loan & Trust Company
Mason City, Iowa

Sam Schneider's death announcement from his bank

Sam Schneider departing, circa 1918

Courtesy of Schlesinger Library,
Radcliffe Institute, Harvard University,
Cornelia Spelman Papers, 2003-M90, Box 1

Half-turned toward the camera, smiling, Sam has a long dimple in one cheek; pronounced eyebrows; a straight, strong nose.

When, as a child, I had asked about him, Mother had said, "Oh, he would have loved you so!" and I had heard in her voice her longing for that love.

In the library's serene main room, its large windows overlooking trees, I scrolled through microfilm of the *Mason City Globe Gazette* for the last few days of November 1918.

The newspaper's pages were filled with details about a vanished world. The armistice ending World War I had just been declared; an Iowa soldier had escaped from a German prison; American soldiers were embarking for home.

The death of a Lieutenant Blettanbergman in an automobile accident had resulted in the revelation that he had two wives, and a controversy had developed between the two women and the military authorities over where the body should be sent for burial.

Men's bathrobes cost $3.95.

Lina Cavalieri was starring in *A Woman of Impulse* at the Bijou Movie Theater. If you ventured to the theater, you were told to wear a mask over your nose and mouth because of the Spanish influenza epidemic.

The twenty-second of November had been cold and clear. The sun had set at 4:36 on November twenty-third.

Seeing events unfold in the newspaper that Sam and Cornie had read, yet knowing, from the future looking back, everything that they could not have known—that the Great War would not be the last world war, that more than six hundred thousand people would die of Spanish influenza in only ten months (Bill Maxwell's mother among them), that Sam had only days left to live—was seeing how we are all trapped in time. What to me was only a distant past had been their present. Time had taken them and those events away, as it would take me and the events of my day. Yet, peering back into their world through those newspapers preserved on film, I was reconnected to them.

When I reached the front page of November 30, 1918, I was startled to see the headline, S. A. SCHNEIDER IS TAKEN BY DEATH: BELOVED CITIZEN AND VICE-PRESIDENT OF THE SECURITY NATIONAL BANK DIES IN CHICAGO THIS MORNING.

The article began:

> The heavy hand of sorrow pressed crushingly down on Mason City this morning when the heart-aching intelligence was received that the bark of optimistic, lovable, generous-hearted Sam A. Schneider had slipped its moorings and that he had gone on the long voyage over the sea whose waves beat on the eternal shores.

What language. The metaphor of Sam as a boat. The "eternal shores." And, yet—the writer had used the words "optimistic," "lovable," and "generous-hearted." The news of Sam's death had been "heart-aching."

The obituary continued,

> One of the choicest spirits this city has ever enjoyed in business and social life; one of the happiest, sunniest, cheeriest souls whose presence has always radiated cheer in any circle or in any group in which he moved; one of the truest, most loyal, most charitable friends man ever enjoyed; one of the most energetic factors in the business life of the community and one of the most thoughtful in his consideration of his fellows whether neighbors, business associates or employees, has waved his farewell and a wife and daughter, a mother, sisters and brothers are crushed with grief and a community of twenty thousand who knew and felt the inspiration of his buoyant spirit, stands too with bowed heads in the presence of a great and genuine sorrow.

Even allowing for the florid prose of a small-town newspaper in 1918, this obituary seemed to express authentic shock and grief, authentic affection. Sam had been called "a buoyant spirit." I read on:

lobe-Gaz

TIMES
D DAILY—TODAY'S NEWS, NOT YESTERD

Y, NOVEMBER 30, 1918.

EACE

PS
TATES

this is
r, there
country
d after
estimate
Leguer.
were An
try are
h Presi-
bidding
Dec. 1.
ko any
ar grain
reweeina
ll have
hile oth
or three
brawer
he have
p going
not nec
after

S. A. SCHNEIDER IS TAKEN BY DEATH

Beloved Citizen and Vice-President of the Security National Bank, Dies in Chicago This Morning.

The heavy hand of sorrow pressed crushingly down on Mason City this morning, when the heart aching intelligence was received that the bark of optimistic, lovable, generous hearted, Sam A. Schneider had slipped its moorings and that he had gone on the long voyage over the sea whose waves beat on the eternal

communl
the next
unable tha
in the nf
numbed.
mystery,
fathom,
the soul
done
Human
forty you
his paren
Schneide
and holy
factors l
caused up
and his
other to
fore com
adyanitng
atjes of C
did work
at Carne
finally u
nd we ca
Bank w
t Titon
tions

The front-page article about Sam's death

Samuel A. Schneider was born forty years ago in October at Garner. His parents were Mr. and Mrs. William Schneider, who were models of piety and holy living and public spirited factors in the community. The deceased spent his boyhood in Garner and his early manhood there and at other towns in Hancock County before coming to Mason City. On September 21, 1907, at Charles City, he was happily married to Miss Cornie White, a popular and charming member of the Mason City High School faculty and one daughter, Elizabeth, came to add to the happiness and joy of the family life, which has been one of rare comradeship of the three members.

The obituary concluded with a poem by Alfred Lord Tennyson, "Crossing the Bar":

> Twilight and evening bell and after that the dark!
> And may there be no sadness of farewell when I
>   embark.
> For though from out our bourne of time and place
>   the flood may bear me far,
> I hope to see my pilot face to face when I have
>   crossed the bar.

Sam had been buried in Elmwood Cemetery, which, the librarian informed me, was the oldest cemetery in Mason City. From the library's pay phone, I telephoned the cemetery office. The woman who answered said, "Sam Schneider? Hold on just a moment." It was as if she were going to get him, to tell him there was a call. She returned to the phone, saying, "He's here. It looks like he's in a plot with room for six others, but he's all alone."

Cornie must have planned to be buried, eventually, with Sam, but then had ended up choosing to be with her parents and sisters in her own hometown, Charles City, thirty miles east. I wondered who the other plots had been intended for.

The cemetery secretary paused, then added, "Money is owed for perpetual care, so I don't know if the stone has been kept up." How could care that was perpetual be dependent on money paid by people who could not, themselves, be perpetual?

Cornie had given meticulous written instructions to Mother about her funeral arrangements, had reminded Mother that she sent flowers to the Episcopal church in Mason City every year on the anniversary of Sam's death. She would have told Mother of the perpetual obligation to Sam's gravestone, but for some reason Mother had neglected it. I wanted to pay what was owed.

It turned out that Elmwood Cemetery was close to my motel, and I arranged to go there the next day. The secretary told me to stop in the office, and the people there would give me a map to Sam's grave.

First, though, I needed to get to the county courthouse to read Sam's probate documents.

In the records office of Mason City's modern courthouse, a thin woman whose intelligent eyes reminded me of Mother put into my hands a stack of documents that she had retrieved from a vault in the basement, labeled "Probate Number 2719."

Requests for records from as long ago as 1918 were not common. The clerk looked curiously at me as she handed over these old papers, and her eyes brightened with interest when I told her of Sam's sudden death, of how my mother had died without ever telling me any details about it.

The clerk led me back into a room with a long wooden table, on which I put the documents and my bag. Large, heavy, gold-embossed leather books, like giant Bibles, too heavy to lift, were all around me on shelves that rolled out on little wheels. Looking inside several books, I saw that they contained handwritten birth, death, and marriage records from Iowa's early years.

I settled down at the table with the stack of Sam's probate documents. Covered by a piece of brown, wrinkled cloth, like the wrapping on a mummy, they were bound with a rubber band so stiff with age it immediately fell apart when I removed it. I wondered if anyone else had looked at these papers since the first of them had been filed in 1918. The rubber band seemed like a link to sunny Sam. I put it in my bag.

Inside the mummylike cloth, folded in thirds, with careful handwritten dates on the outside, was a neat, narrow stack of documents about six inches tall. Looking around first to see if anyone was watching me, I bent my head to sniff them. I don't know what I had expected, but they didn't smell like anything—just old, dry, paper.

One of the documents was an inventory of Sam's estate. Because he had died without a will, Cornie had been required to record every item that they owned, including their household furnishings.

The inventory listed a Hudson Super-Six touring car and a Paige roadster, twelve rugs, eighteen chairs, five beds with bedding, six dining room chairs, a davenport, a piano, a dining room table and buffet, a sewing table, two library tables, three desks, three dressers, three chiffoniers, a cedar chest, and a Victrola with records—as well as dishes and silverware, wearing apparel, pictures, and small household articles. Sam also owned real estate and some bank stocks.

Three bills had been submitted to the estate: $27.35 from an Elmer E. Russell, dated June 2, 1918, for "repairing windshield, adjusting brakes and helping get touring car out of mud 10 hours." I wondered if it had been Sam, or Cornie, who had gotten the car stuck in the mud, only a few months before Sam died, and whether they had laughed or argued about it. I wondered why they hadn't paid the bill.

There was a bill from the Hathorn Auto Company for $4.10 for gasoline and a car wash on November 20, 1918—the day before they left on their last trip. And finally, there was a bill from a Fred Randall for a burial vault ($125) and the rental of a hearse and three autos ($27).

Cornie's distinctive signature was on many of the papers. On the earliest ones, immediately after Sam's death, her graceful, firm writing was noticeably smaller and cramped, as if from the weight of her grief and shock. Over the years, her signature grew larger and more confident.

The documents began in 1918 and ended when Mother reached adulthood in 1932. They were arranged chronologically,

In the District Court of the State of Iowa, in and for Cerro Go.

IN THE MATTER OF THE ESTATE OF

Samuel A. Schneider.
_____
Deceased.

INVENTORY

Come...now the undersigned.....Administratrix
and state..s...that the following is a true, correct and complete inventory of
ceased which have come to the knowledge of said ....administra

PROPERTY OF DECEASED REGARDED AS E

Number of Articles	ARTICLES (All articles, including household furniture, must be listed
1	Super-six Hudson Touring Car
12	Rugs.
5	Beds with bedding.
6	Dining Room chairs.
18	Chairs.
1	Davenport
1	Piano
1	Dining Room table.
1	Buffet.
1	Sewing Table.
2	Library Tables.
3	Desks
3	Dressers
3	Chiffoniers
1	Cedar Chest
	Dishes and Silverware.
1	Victrola with records
2	Tables
	Wearing Apparel
	Pictures

The inventory of Sam and Cornie's household goods, 1919

so that by reading them I could, in a way, follow Cornie and Mother's life together after Sam's death.

The estate must not have been enough to support them—or else Cornie spent too much—because she kept returning to the court asking for permission to sell more real estate or stocks or to take out loans.

In 1925, when Mother was fourteen, Cornie sold their beautiful home at 525 East State Street.

In 1929, after the stock market crash, Cornie petitioned the court for loans to pay Mother's tuition and expenses at the University of Illinois.

In 1932, when Mother reached the age of twenty-one and was entitled to receive two-thirds of her father's estate, Cornie stated to the court that "the property which remains is not adequate to pay the interest that would be coming to Elizabeth Schneider."

Also in 1932, Cornie, who had remained a widow all the years after Sam died, married again, to a rich man whose proposal she had rejected before she had ever married Sam.

I took a picture of the documents before I handed them back to the bright-eyed clerk. She promised to keep them out of the vault another day in case I wanted to return.

Then I went back to the library to meet the local historian, a courtly, genial man in his seventies who had grown up in Mason City. He had thoughtfully obtained for me a copy of Mother's high school yearbook and had arranged to take me to meet, most improbably, Mother's teacher, Miss Reta Spooner.

When we entered the Good Shepherd Health Center, where Miss Spooner lived, it was as if we had gone underwater. Some of the residents moved so slowly, if they moved at all, that it was as if they were pushing against a strong, invisible current.

My escort stopped to chat with several of the elderly residents he was acquainted with who were sitting in the common area, and we made our way toward the room of Mother's teacher.

In her yearbook photo, Miss Reta Spooner was a smiling young woman, only a few years older than her students, with an open and direct gaze. I could not recognize that young face in the ancient one of the wheelchair-bound woman to whom I was introduced. I was in the presence of tenacious life.

I shook Miss Spooner's frail hand gently. Explaining that I was the daughter of her student, who had died many years ago, I handed her Mother's senior photo and asked whether she remembered her.

Miss Spooner looked at Mother's photo with concentration, then turned her face quizzically back to mine, as if she were seeing a ghost. A deep red flush spread up beneath the fragile skin of her face. Her mouth began to tremble, and tears spilled down her cheeks. I was afraid I had stabbed this elderly lady with the news that Mother, whom she would have remembered only as a fresh-faced young girl, was long dead. But perhaps her tears were only due to her extreme age.

When Miss Spooner's mouth stopped trembling, she looked searchingly at me, then back at the photograph. But after all of that, all she said was, "Your mother was an outstanding student." I stayed for a few more moments, hoping for something else, but that was all Miss Spooner could offer.

I was glad to leave the Good Shepherd, with its complex odor of cooked food, disinfectant, and floor polish. It reminded me of the place where Mother had died.

Later, I stopped at the Congregational church, an Italian Romanesque limestone building with a tall bell tower, where Sam's funeral had been held. This was the church where Meredith Willson, the composer of *The Music Man*, had attended Sunday school.

I sat down on one of the curving wood pews in the vaulted main room, which was illuminated by massive stained-glass windows. It was a large church, which was why the funeral had been held here instead of at the small Episcopal church that Sam and Cornie had attended.

I had read that a quarantine due to Spanish influenza had stopped church services for some weeks in October of 1918. Yet the newspaper said a "large concourse of friends, the Elks lodge attending in a body" had flocked here for Sam's funeral on that cold December second. His obituary had informed me that Sam had been a member of Mason City's Chamber of Commerce, Rotary Club, Masonic Temple, the Knights of Pythias, and the Modern Brotherhood of America, and there were representatives of all of those clubs at the funeral. As a banker in this fast-growing town of "twenty thousand souls" and a native of the area, Sam had known a lot of people.

This church where I was sitting had been filled with all those people, with the fragrances of the flowers they must have sent. I imagined Sam's childhood friend, who had written about his death in his hometown paper, speaking that day at the funeral, his voice ringing up to the hushed people in the second-floor balcony:

> Old time friends of Sam Schneider, and they are numerous here, were shocked Saturday by the intelligence that he had died. No one here knew he was ailing and the news was well nigh unbelievable. My acquaintance with Sam A. Schneider extends over a period of more than thirty years. Our boyhood homes were just across the street from each other, and for more than a decade of years we were pals. I knew his boyhood secrets, told him mine, and as a verification of what the Globe-Gazette editor wrote, not even my boyhood confidence in him was betrayed. I have with me a mind-picture of Sam as a boy. I recall the thousands of pranks in which we were jointly implicated, but these memories, pleasant as they would be if our friend was alive, have been turned to sorrow by his death. My feelings are but the reflections of the entire population of Garner for we all liked Sam.

Somewhere near where I sat had stood Sam's brothers, Daniel and Benjamin, and his friend Julius Kunz. Cornie had been here, with her sister, Maude, and her parents Genevieve and Herbert White. Seven-year-old Mother had been here.

Emerging from my reverie I noticed a side altar, the words "holy, holy, holy" written in gold leaf across its front. Among Mother's papers after she had died was an essay titled "An

Autobiography of Prayer," which she had written, when she was fifty-four, for a graduate school class at the Episcopal Diocese of Boston. She writes about a recurring dream she had had years after she had stopped going to church, which she interpreted to mean that she ought to return to religion:

> I had a recurring dream in which I saw the little brown wooden altar of my childhood parish, with its gilt "Holy, Holy, Holy" printed across the front. Before the altar was a huge pile of stones and rubble, and over this hurdle I was compelled to crawl, with great effort and considerable discomfort to hands and knees. As soon as I had negotiated one difficult area, another even larger pile appeared.

Decades later, sitting in front of what could be the altar Mother had dreamed about, with its "holy, holy, holy" across the front, I wondered whether her dream images were her buried memories of her anguish at her father's funeral here in this church, and of his burial in Elmwood Cemetery.

If only Mother had sought help for her grief, like her old friend Bill had. If only she had shed those tears. Perhaps she wouldn't have ended up the way she did.

The clean pastor in his crisp, ironed shirt told me that the church was now used for community programs. There had been arrests the week before for methamphetamine sales and use. Drug dealers used the tidy, small Mason City airport, and a bullet had pierced the window of Sam's old Masonic Lodge. What a fantasy I had had, that old Iowa would have somehow been preserved for me.

Early that evening, spring snow came. When I looked out my motel window, the green rental car had a dusting of sparkling white. Not far from my room, somewhere in Elmwood Cemetery, it was snowing on Sam's grave. Falling asleep, I heard a train whistle—I fancied it was the train I had boarded carrying me back to the past.

I woke early. Outside the motel's thin rubber-backed curtains, the sun poured over the prairie—what was left of the prairie. Across the street was a huge discount store surrounded by a Red Square–sized lot of concrete. Both sides of this stretch of highway outside Mason City were strip malls. I had read that when the pioneers, including Mother's great-grandparents, had arrived in this area, the prairies "like some wide expanding carpet of emerald, were literally covered with flowers."

But Iowa's farms had been steadily disappearing, and many towns' economies had declined. The previous afternoon, on my way back to the library, I had parked in the old downtown, which had been severed in two by the strip malls. I had wandered past a once-handsome apartment building, the Kirk, Sam and Cornie's first home as newlyweds. Its copper-clad bays and cornices had turned green. The Park Inn Hotel, designed by Frank Lloyd Wright, was boarded up on the second floor, the first floor now occupied only by a few shops. The only other person I had seen on the street was a shuffling, shaggy-haired old man.

The people I had come in contact with were polite and friendly, but I wondered whether it was dispiriting to live where there was no longer a real downtown. Mason City had once been an important place. Now it felt stranded, without enough opportunities. At my solitary dinner in one of the strip-mall restaurants, the strong young waitress seemed eager to talk with me. While I was answering her questions about what I was doing there, she hungrily eyed my polished nails, my clothes. She said that she, too, would like to write about her family. She was not, she said, even from Mason City, the big city around here, but from a town west of it—"a speck on the map."

After checking out of the motel the next morning I went to Elmwood Cemetery, which was marked by an imposing stone gate and stately trees. I got the map from the office, then drove slowly down the cemetery's narrow road, crunching the gravel beneath my wheels, to Lot 17, Block 4, Second Addition, where I parked and got out of the car. The snow had melted.

After a few moments of wandering, I found it. A dappled, gray marble stone, rough on the sides and polished on its face and top, tilting slightly after seventy-nine years, stood not far from a tree—a tree so large that it must have been a silent witness when grieving friends, family, a young widow, and a little girl named Tidie had buried Sam beneath it.

Sam was, as the cemetery secretary had told me, "all alone" in the plot. I got the idea that I might move Mother's remains here to be with him—might finally reunite her with her father. But what difference would it make to anyone but me? And why disturb the dead? The stone was engraved with a simple border and the words, SAMUEL A. SCHNEIDER 1878–1918. As I bent over to trace Sam's name with my finger, my eyes filled with tears.

12

1918

Not long after I returned home from that trip to Mason City, I received an envelope from my oldest sister in Amsterdam. Inside it, folded for so long its creases were nearly torn, was a letter on stationery from St. Luke's Hospital in Chicago. It exactly fit into that empty envelope from St. Luke's that I had found among Mother's papers. Handwritten from Cornie to her seven-year-old daughter, the letter contained the last piece of information that I needed to know. Finally, I could imagine the whole story of Sam's death.

In the late afternoon of Thursday, November 21, 1918, a week before Thanksgiving and ten days after the armistice ending World War I had been signed, Sam and Cornie Schneider locked the back door of their Prairie style house on East State Street overlooking Willow Creek in Mason City, Iowa, stowed their suitcases in their black Hudson Super-Six touring car, and with their only child—seven-year-old Elizabeth, nicknamed "Tidie"—drove thirty miles east, past wintry dun-colored fields, to Cornie's parents' house in Charles City, Iowa.

Sam and Cornie were taking Tidie to stay with her grandparents, Herbert and Genevieve White, before getting on the train to travel on to French Lick Springs, Indiana, a popular resort, for what the *Mason City Globe-Gazette* later said was to have been a "short recuperative rest."

Sam and Cornie's house,
designed by Walter Burley Griffin circa 1915,
at 525 East State Street, Mason City, Iowa

Sam and Cornie would be taking the Chicago, Milwaukee, & St. Paul Railway's night train to Chicago, where they would make connections to French Lick Springs. The train left Charles City at 8:42 P.M., and they had booked a sleeping car, as it wasn't due to arrive in Chicago until 8:15 the next morning.

They planned to be back to celebrate Thanksgiving at "the White house on the hill," the white clapboard home of the White family on Gilbert Street in Charles City, in which Cornie and her sisters, Maude and Edna, had been born and Tidie's great-grandparents had died. In its parlor, decorated with autumn flowers on a September day eleven years earlier, Sam and Cornie had been married.

Large and comfortable, the center-gabled White house faced a lawn sloping down to the Cedar River. Tall elms lined the long walk from its front door to the street. Inside, a flowered carpet warmed the parlor and dining room, and heavy drapes at the doorways kept out drafts.

Tidie had often visited her grandparents' home and was familiar with the stack of sheet music piled next to the darkly gleaming, ornate Story and Clark upright piano; the chaise longue piled cozily with pillows and throws; the painting of sea and lighthouse; and the portrait of her mother Cornie as a child that hung from the parlor's picture rail.

Tidie's grandmother Genevieve kept photos of her three daughters in an oval gold frame on top of her walnut secretary desk. There was a photograph of Tidie, about two years old, dressed in a satin coat, hat, shoes, and muff. The expression in her large, hazel, almond-shaped eyes was solemn. She was the only grandchild in this family of three sisters.

The White home on Gilbert Street was that of a well-established family. Genevieve's parents had helped settle Charles City in the 1850s. Tidie's grandfather, Herbert White, was the proprietor of the Elm Street Creamery. An excellent cheese and butter maker, he had won a medal at the American Centennial of 1876. Herbert had served as the sheriff of Floyd County.

Cornie's parents' home, the White house on the hill,
at 812 Gilbert Street in Charles City, Iowa, circa 1907

Looking into the dining room inside the White house

Cornie and Sam, Tidie and her grandparents—she called them Dampoo and Nonnie—sat down to dinner together. Cornie's oldest sister, Edna, thirty-eight, still lived at home, and was very ill with lymphoma. Childless herself, Edna was very fond of her only niece.

Maude, thirty-seven, the middle sister—Tidie called her Mun—lived in Chicago. Maude was divorced from a man who had become an opium addict. He had managed a salmon factory in Alaska, and Maude enjoyed shocking people with tales of Alaskan opium dens. A fun-loving, boisterous woman with a talent for playing the piano by ear, Maude had recently returned from entertaining the troops overseas.

During dinner, Tidie looked up at the plate rail where Genevieve kept a few pieces of her pink-and-purple Spode china and a flowered china clock Tidie wasn't allowed to touch. She ran her fingers over the smooth, cool, mother-of-pearl handles of Genevieve's silver dinner knives while the adults talked about the armistice, the soldiers—friends and neighbors—who would be coming home, and Spanish influenza.

After dinner, Cornie got Tidie ready for bed. She took off the large satin ribbon holding Tidie's long, dark hair, curled into ringlets at her shoulders, and helped her into her nightgown.

When she was ready for bed, Sam came in to read to her. Tidie loved "Escape at Bedtime" from Robert Louis Stevenson's *A Child's Garden of Verses*, and more than forty years later, when she put me to bed, she could still recite it by heart:

> The lights from the parlor and kitchen shone out
> Through the blinds and the windows and bars;
> And high overhead and all moving about,
> There were thousands of millions of stars.
> There ne'er were such thousands of leaves on a tree,
> Nor of people in church or the Park,
> As the crowds of the stars that looked down upon me,
> And that glittered and winked in the dark.
> The Dog, and the Plough, and the Hunter and all,
> And the star of the sailor, and Mars,
> These shone in the sky, and the pail by the wall

Would be half full of water and stars.
They saw me at last, and they chased me with cries,
And they soon had me packed into bed,
But the glory kept shining and bright in my eyes,
And the stars going round in my head.

Sam kissed and hugged his young daughter before he tucked her into bed with her doll, Barbara. He and Cornie were only going to be gone for six days, but still, it was hard for Tidie to say good-bye. Other fathers had gone away to war and never come back. Everyone was talking about Spanish influenza. Tidie knew that bad things could happen to people—she knew, even though her grandparents and parents tried not to show it, that they were worried and sad about Edna. So, even though she was doted upon by Dampoo and Nonnie and Edna, Tidie didn't want her mother and father to leave her.

If she cried, she probably didn't cry very long. She was expected to be a little adult. Except by Sam. Tidie's comfort in him, and his tenderness for her, are apparent in a photograph from the summer of 1918, in which she's lying outdoors on the grass, her head resting in Sam's lap as he gazes intently down at her, smiling.

She looks sure of her place, in Sam's lap.

Sam didn't like good-byes, either. He had had to part, forever, from someone he loved. His first wife, twenty-year-old Edith, a postal clerk from his hometown of Garner, Iowa, had died of the "white death"—tuberculosis—only eight months after their wedding. Sam's marriage to Cornie five years later, and then Tidie's birth, had brought him a happiness he had thought might never be his.

But Sam and Cornie were looking forward to their trip. They were belatedly celebrating Sam's fortieth birthday, which had fallen the month before. They were celebrating the end of the war and their overall good fortune. For, despite the war, despite the Spanish influenza, despite Edna's sickness, life had been good to them and was promising to be even better. Had the song "Summertime" been written, it could have been Tidie's song, for her daddy was rich and her mama good-looking.

Mother with her head in Sam's lap, 1918

Cornie, thirty-four, had wavy, light-brown hair, clear hazel eyes, a tall, shapely figure, and even, white, gleaming teeth. Artistic, she had been a teacher of art and handwriting in the Mason City Public Schools before her marriage, and it was her interest in the new Prairie school architecture that had persuaded Sam to hire the Chicago architect Walter Burley Griffin to design their house, completed three years earlier.

Sam, an ambitious businessman and officer of two banks, was among those profiting from a period of intense growth in Mason City, which in 1918 was the most important city for a hundred miles.

Sam was also good-looking. Six feet tall, slim, with dark, curly hair and merry brown eyes, he had an engaging smile that caused a long dimple in one cheek. And he was playful. A photograph of him as a young man shows him, although dressed in a three-piece suit, cuddled up with his arm around a laughing male friend. Because of his optimism, friendliness, and wide smile, his nickname was Sunny Sam.

About eight o'clock on that Thursday night, with Tidie asleep, Sam and Cornie said farewell to Edna and Genevieve, and Herbert drove them to the one-story brick train depot on Grand Avenue in Charles City.

Just on time, the train slowed and stopped at the depot. After picking up its new passengers and the mail, it chugged on through the cold night air of the prairie, its bright headlight cutting through the darkness.

In their darkened sleeping compartment, on one of the narrow berths, Sam and Cornie lay together, their arms around each other, talking softly for a while as the train rocked its way across the prairie past Fort Atkinson, where Cornie's mother had been born.

They were asleep when the train passed through the towns of Ossian, and Monona, sometimes sounding its melancholy whistle; asleep when it crossed the great Mississippi River, on which Sam's mother had traveled to Iowa from New Orleans, after immigrating from Germany as a young woman.

Sam and Cornie, April 15, 1909

Courtesy of Schlesinger Library, Radcliffe Institute,
Harvard University, Cornelia Spelman Papers, 2003-M90, Box 1

Sam and a friend clowning, circa 1902

But at some point in the early morning hours, Sam was awake and in pain.

By the time the train arrived in Chicago at 8:15 on Friday morning, November 22, Sam had to be rushed off, through the echoing station to an ambulance that took him to St. Luke's Hospital on South Michigan Avenue.

At St. Luke's, the chief of surgery, Dr. Lewis Linn McArthur, educated in Heidelberg and Vienna, recognized by his peers as "a brilliant operator, a man of originality and excellent judgment" diagnosed appendicitis and arranged to operate at once. Despite the risks of surgery, it was the only chance to save Sam's life.

Back in Iowa, in response to Cornie's call, Sam's old friend Julius Kunz hurried onto a train and traveled to St. Luke's to be with them. Maude had already hastened to St. Luke's from her apartment in Chicago.

Saturday, November 23; Sunday, November 24; Monday, November 25; Tuesday, November 26—the days came and went.

Finally, on Wednesday, November 27—nearly a week after Sam and Cornie had departed on the night train—Julius and Cornie telephoned anxious family and friends in Iowa to give them the good news that Sam would recover.

On Thursday, Thanksgiving, anticipating that she and Sam would not be able to return home for some weeks, Cornie asked Maude to travel out to Iowa to take Tidie back to her home and school in Mason City, and to send some of Cornie's clothes. She wrote Maude a list of things to do for her:

> *Phone Ann and ask how much I owe her and if she still wants me to look for coat—*
>
> *Phone Beth and some of the girls—tell them (Beth—Pres. of club) I will not be back until about Xmas—*
>
> *My Dorum skirt—with pockets—Clean underclothes in drawer in your room—2nd drawer—Hat and mole neckpiece—pumps—new of them—bedroom slippers*

St. Luke's Hospital's Smith Memorial, built in 1907.
Sam was taken there for surgery in 1918.

Courtesy of Rush University Medical Center Archives

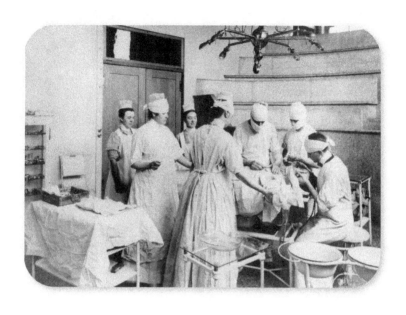

Surgery, St. Luke's Hospital, 1913
Courtesy of Rush University Medical Center Archives

Dear dear little "Judie"

Papa is better today and the Dr feels he is getting along fine. Auntie Mun will bring your doll furniture & Mass book home with her. How is Baby Barbara? When I have more time I will look up some other things for her.

Have Auntie Mun wash your Collars & cuffs on Wool jersey dress in Lux

Cornie's letter to Mother from
St. Luke's Hospital, November 1918

And she gave Maude a note for Tidie, who had been waiting all these days so far away:

Dear dear little Tidie,

Papa is better today and the Dr. feels he is getting along fine.

Auntie Mun will bring your doll furniture & Mass book home with her. How is Baby Barbara? When I have more time I will look up some other things for her.

Have Auntie Mun wash your collars and cuffs on wool jersey dress in Lux and you can wear any of your three dresses to school.

I want mentholatum up your nose every day & take Castoria when needed. Auntie Mun will go to M. City with you & mother & Daddy will hurry home—

And we have much to be thankful for that Papa is gaining. When we come home we will have our turkey together.

Next week I will look up the spats etc. & have Mun try them on you also some pumps.

Give Dampoo & Nonnie my love & be a good little girl & <u>do not</u> eat candy.

Oceans of love from Mother

But on Saturday, November 30, at one o'clock in the morning, Sam's kidneys began failing. Cornie and Julius were at his side when, at twenty-one minutes past four in the morning, Sam died.

Early the next morning, Cornie and Julius accompanied Sam's coffin back to Mason City on the train.

Seven-year-old Tidie was waiting at home with her Aunt Maude. She stood, holding on to Maude, as her father's coffin was carried into their home for a private family service.

She stood, later, stunned, at Sam's public funeral at the Congregational church. And stunned, afterward, at Elmwood Cemetery, when, in the shadow of an elm tree, Sam's coffin was lowered into the ground.

13

After a Lifetime of Silence

In 1974, Mother died the day after Thanksgiving. Because the calendar date of Thanksgiving changes every year, I wasn't sure of the actual date. I wrote away to get a copy of her death certificate.

I learned that she had died on November 29—only seven hours away from the exact moment of her father Sam's death on November 30, 1918. It was beyond coincidence. The timing of her death seemed an eloquent statement, after a lifetime of silence, about what his loss had meant to her.

14

Oceans of Love

Cornie signed that letter to her young daughter from St. Luke's Hospital "oceans of love." So it seems she was capable of being warm. Perhaps it was Sam's death—and her sister Edna's, only weeks later—that turned Cornie into the cold and critical mother she later became, the materialistic woman Mother later described to me as caring more for things than people.

Cornie didn't remarry until 1932, the same year Mother and Pop married. Her stepson, who was fourteen when she married his father and who lived in the same town with her for twenty-five years, until her death, told me that, though she could show considerable charm, she was "remote." She and his father would go to Miami Beach in the winters, leaving him at home with the housekeeper, the furniture covered in dust sheets.

It could not have been easy for Mother, an only child, to grow up without a father and with a mother who was remote. Photos of her as a child show her extremely dressed up—Cornie's beautiful little doll.

But a daughter, unlike a doll, grows up, and might fall in love with and marry someone her mother does not like; she becomes an individual with her own ideas.

In 1962, Cornie wrote her fifty-one-year old daughter:

Mother, when she was Cornie's little doll, circa 1912

Dear Tidie,

*Your letter came yesterday and I was glad to hear you had a
nice trip home in spite of my being ill for I am sorry but I was
ill just looking at you. Well if it takes seven months to get that
awful silver out of your hair it must be pretty strong stuff and
so I will make up my mind not to see you again for some time.
If I am still alive at that time. I am nearly seventy-eight and
anything might happen—and if it does before then I wouldn't
see you or know how you looked.*

*I am not going to Rochester [the Mayo Clinic] I will
stay home and take the pills as I have done right along.
If I last until fall I will go up at my usual time. It really
doesn't matter I am ready to go anytime I miss Maude and
all my family and will be glad to join them. I am not much
interested in anything anymore. I love you very much and
I feel I have neglected you and your family but the family
do not really know me or I them. There are a few things you
should know in my letter to you which is here in my desk
with also my arrangements for my funeral, where my keys
are, etc.*

*I have many valuable things here—an oriental rug in
basement priced at $800—the teak wood table in living
room, which ought to bring $500. I have fourteen pieces of
LaChanel pottery—blue-green—and as the place in France
where it came from has burned down . . . my mink coat is
in New York at DunBachers—my sable scarf, hat and sable
cape at Bicha's fur place for storage, here in La Crosse—
many of Mother's things are here, tables, etc.*

*All the cut glass was given to us by Mr. Potter when
Sam and I were married 55 years ago—many things for
you to sort over and dispose of—sorry I have so much, but
it is all good. Of course when I die the trust fund in Miami
Beach will stop, so my income will be cut in half. I could
go on and on about other things but why worry you—I send
my love to all.*

Mother

"The family do not really know me, or I them," Cornie wrote, as if she had nothing to do with that. But in the summer of 1946, a few months before my birth, Mother had written her:

Dearest Duchess,

Was very glad to get your letter, although I was disturbed by its tone. I don't mean what you had to say about the new baby, because, as I said, that was what is known as an Act of God, and there's nothing to be done or said about it anyhow, and I do feel perfectly straightened out in my own mind about it—but I mean about the tone of your letters in general for maybe the last two years or so, the change that seems to have come about in our relationship.

In whatever I have to say now—and I've mulled this over and over and feel that I really must say something about it—I don't want you to feel in any way, shape or form any real or implied criticism of you, because I blame myself very bitterly for being at fault. It's a thing that's been on my conscience for a long long time, and I can't put off any longer trying to get it all straight.

I'm sure that in some way—and probably a good many ways—I have been a sad failure as a daughter. I believe most sincerely in ultimate justice, and I have no doubt whatever that I shall be punished for that failure. It will probably be connected with [my own child] in some fashion or other, . . . but most of all I am punished for it by being deprived of the relationship that should exist between you and me. In any event, I should like to do anything in my power to set it right, and first of all I'd like to understand it a little better.

I know of course that you and I disagree about a good many things, but, after all, those seem to me to be pretty superficial things—politics and such, which certainly, so far as I am concerned, and I hope so far as you are concerned too, are not the basic things in any family

relationship. But your letters seem to me more like
those that you'd write to a casual acquaintance, and
of course that is a hurting sort of thing, and I wish I
could do something to set it right.

Perhaps I've forfeited already whatever right I
had to anything else, but I hope not. When I am
so deeply happy in my own family life, it makes me
most unhappy that you shouldn't want to share in it,
as I would so like you to do. I can't tell you what it
would mean to me to have you know and love your
grandchildren, and to come and see us sometimes. Surely
it can't be too late for that, or for you to feel
so far removed from us that you don't want to. That I
simply can't believe, and I feel, as I said before, that it
must in some way be my fault.

Maybe I've been too careless or thoughtless or busy
to say the things I should have said, but if so, please
consider them said now. I'm not, as a matter of fact,
awfully good at that sort of thing, but please do know
that my heart and my home are open to you whenever
you want to avail yourself of them. My life seems so rich
to me that the only thing lacking in it is your not sharing
it as much as we'd all like you to.

I hope all this won't sound silly to you. I repeat, I've
gone over and over it so many times in my own mind, and
I would so like to put it all down much more ably, but I
hope you'll understand, and that, if there is anything in
my power to do to set it right, you'll let me do it.

All my love,
Tidie

In the letter, Mother expresses guilt about her imagined failings as a daughter, unable to recognize that the fault lay not with her but with a mother incapable of love. And Mother's religious beliefs fueled her sense of guilt. Every Sunday in church she would recite the prayer known as the General Confession:

Almighty God, Father of our Lord Jesus Christ, Maker of all things, Judge of all men; we acknowledge and bewail our manifold sins and wickedness, which we, from time to time, most grievously have committed, by thought, word, and deed, against Thy Divine Majesty, provoking most justly Thy wrath and indignation against us. We do earnestly repent, and are heartily sorry for these our misdoings. The remembrance of them is grievous unto us, the burden of them is intolerable.

Wanting to know all I could about Mother's childhood and her relationship with Cornie, I pored over a diary she kept in 1925, when she was fourteen. She feared that if she failed to live up to her mother's standards of behavior, Cornie would "have spasms," "go straight up," or give her "Hail, Columbia." She made a New Year's resolution to "be awfully nice to Mother." Cornie woke Tidie up to tell her, Tidie wrote, that "someone had said terrible things about me, I was wild, etc. and she had worried so she just had to tell me. Mother worries about one thing or another most of the time and her worrying kind of worries me."

Tidie sneaked out the back door of a church group meeting, kissed a boy, and smoked a cigarette. But, "Someone told Mother about last night (she won't tell me who) and I am chastened, humbled and heartily ashamed! I asked God for help last night and to show me what was right and He did in this way. And I thank Him that he did. After this I'm going to play fair—for it wasn't playing fair to Mother to do what I did. Oh gee it seems life's just one big struggle and a hard one at that—can't a girl be good and yet be a flapper?"

But Tidie and Cornie had some times of closeness, too. Tidie wrote, "I had a keen talk with Mother today and I somehow feel a lot closer to her. I found a keen article in a magazine about mothers and daughters and I read it to Mother and we had a fine talk. She even admitted she used to spoon. Can you imagine? (Human nature doesn't change though I guess.) And she said that it was all right to let a fellow put his arm around you and kiss you just so he doesn't go farther. Gee, I can sure pet with a clearer conscience now (if I ever get another chance). Mother is

Mother striking a pose as a teenager, circa 1927

Courtesy of Schlesinger Library, Radcliffe Institute, Harvard University, Cornelia
Spelman Papers, 2003-M90, Box 1

doing her best to be a good sport with me and so I think it's only fair to try to be a good scout with her. I'm gonna stay home and try to do things with her a little now."

One night when Tidie was feeling "terribly spooky," she reported, "Mother is gonna sleep with me." And she wrote "I am popular with girls but boys—well, I'm a complete flop with everybody but Jimmy and I don't <u>want</u> him." But "Mother said tonight though that a woman told her that I was stunning and aristocratic looking and tall girls can wear their clothes so that helps."

At the end of the school year in 1925, Tidie wrote, "The house is sold. I'm really quite sick about it but Mother mustn't know I am because she feels dreadful herself."

Cornie even confided to her daughter that a Mr. Smith was in love with her. Tidie's response was loyal: "It's a darn shame that he's tied up to that wife of his. Oh, heck, he ought to be my step-papa."

In 1927, still only sixteen, Tidie graduated from high school and left home for the University of Illinois. After three and a half years at the university, she completed her undergraduate work and enrolled in a master's program in English. That summer she wrote a poem for Cornie's forty-seventh birthday:

I saw you once across a crowded room where candles
    glittered,
Casting faint, warm gleams of yellow light on silver,
    on the sheen of yellow roses, and rich, dim tapestry.
Serene you sat, and gracious; firm proud chin held high,
    and in one small white hand you clasped a fragile,
    milk-white tea cup.
And I thought, "The essence of her life lies in this room,
    in these dark panels, and that deep blue rug,
This polished silver, that burnished copper vase—
A sheltered life, apart, above the rest."

In early 1932, when Tidie wrote her congratulations to Cornie upon her remarriage, she called her "my best love."

Cornie's second marriage obtained for her that "sheltered

life, apart, above the rest." She lived as if the Depression didn't exist. In her papers, I found a newspaper clipping in which a society reporter described the Surf Club in Miami Beach, to which she and her new husband belonged:

> Never have I seen anything like the breath-taking elegance of the place—the great lounges, the high-vaulted dining rooms, the dance patios, pool, blue-and-gold mirrored terrace bar, the Mediterranean cafe, the curving line of 235 double-decked cabanas on the ocean front. We lunched in what I suspect must be the world's swankiest cafeteria. Everything from imported caviar to Baked Alaska. Behind each dish, a stiffly uniformed attendant; others to carry each guest's tray along the line; a maitre de cafeteria to make suggestions about the terrapin and jellied fowl. Wine stewards; proletarian beer bottles glorified in pristine napery and silver champagne buckets. Patio and palms. A ten-piece orchestra.

Meanwhile, in Kansas City, Mother and Pop were living a very different sort of life. Bill Maxwell sent me a letter he had found that Pop had written to him in September 1934:

Dear Billie,

The state of my typewriter ribbon speaks louder and with more force than the words I was going to use later in this letter to tell you of our sour-did financial state, but that part over with, I may embark on the motif proper. It is, of course, your book, Bright Center of Heaven *the which we saw a review of it in last week's* Herald Tribune. *I'm reviewing books for the* Star, *and have fenny dibs on yours if it comes in. Mr. Louis Mecker, known to the irreverent as Miss Louise Mecker, literary and serial editor, says he gets very few books from* Harper's. *The reason is as plain as could be: the* Star, *which is a great paper, is very piddling as regards culcher, and is less sympathetic with publishers than with the gangsters.*

There are more gangsters, to be sure, but as the Star *is the organ of the Artistic Civic and Cultural capital of the Southwest, in strict alphabetical order, it should be a little more lavish.*

I haven't the faintest idea where this will find you. Since the ignorance is probably mutual, I'll avail myself of this opportunity which is plenty availing with a damnable old Corona like this, to answer your letter of some eighteen months ago, wishing us well.

We are well, thanks to the minor gods who brood over chumps. I took a job which blew up in June, and have been devoting myself until a week ago to that fragrant vagueness known as "earning a living by the pen." Earning a living my ass, if I may say so. Due to the kindness of a wealthy lady we are living in a reconditioned whorehouse, sharing a bath with a German portrait painter who pees on the floor. . . .

The Star *has taken a few features and some very good people have refused a lot more, so I'm back in the mortgage business for a while. I'm trying some radio continuity too, with puns which I hope Bob Henderson hears some day.*

Elizabeth will write you, I think, although most of her writing is unbelievably ingenious notes to the awful number of people getting married, explaining why we aren't sending a present. She wishes me to say she loves you, however. She is content, I think: we're trying to work some way so she can go to art school this fall, to learn drawing so she can make cartoons. Our neighborhood is rich in subtitle stuff if we could only draw the people. I had hoped to make this longer: it seems to me there was quite a little more to say, but the machine has got me down. Let me hear from you.

But Pop did not manage to earn a living by the pen, nor did Mother make it to art school. Instead, a year after that letter, they had their first child—Frank—and Cornie's husband had to give Pop a job.

126

Pop and Mother, circa 1933

*Mother and Cornie on the steps of the Surf Club,
Miami Beach, Florida, circa 1944*

Over the following dozen years, the interests of mother and daughter continued to diverge. While Cornie attended balls at the Surf Club—one photo shows her wearing an ivory velvet cape with a chinchilla collar—Mother had three more children, which Pop could not have supported without Cornie's husband's help.

Cornie did not approve of Pop. She did not approve of large families. She did not approve of Mother's housekeeping, or of her enthusiasm for FDR.

On a visit Mother made to Cornie in Miami Beach, a photograph was taken of the two women standing on the Surf Club's outdoor stairs. Mother and daughter are wearing sparkly pins. Cornie's is shaped like a fish, Mother's like a bird. Mother looks strained and uncomfortable in her mother's world. A fish, and a bird, unable to breathe in each other's space.

Cornie's husband died ten years after their marriage, leaving her well off. During his final illness he had told his son, "If I could get rid of that woman, I would." Mother continued to travel yearly to Wisconsin to see Cornie in the handsome five-bedroom house where she lived alone, served by a housekeeper, cook, and yard man.

When Cornie was in her final illness, Mother wrote me,

> I'm going to La Crosse tomorrow and dreading every minute of it. Cornie is very confused mentally and one moment she's pleasant and the next minute damning everyone. Yesterday she telephoned me and said not to come, she didn't want me there now. But of course I have to go anyhow—they're having much trouble with nurses and I'll have to help out that way whether she likes it or not. So it all sounds jolly, no? No. I'll call you sometime from there. In the meantime, drop me a note and cheer me up!

Cornie died alone. Tucked into an envelope addressed "Elizabeth—to be opened at once upon my death," with her instructions for various arrangements, was a yellowed newspaper clipping with this poem:

A daughter is a lovely gift
Who brings so much of pleasure
Throughout the years
Through smiles and tears
She is a blessed treasure.
A daughter is a precious gem
Adds luster to our living
Makes dreams come true
And keeps them new
A cause for real Thanksgiving.

15

A Sort of Glad, Wild Song

In the late 1920s, when Mother and Pop and Bill Maxwell were friends at the University of Illinois, the campus looked like a college movie set, with an ivy-covered brick College of Arts and Sciences and a central common, known as the Broadwalk, canopied with elms and lit by globe-topped lampposts.

Only a few years before she met Pop, Mother had written of a boy in her girlhood diary:

> *He was so adorable! Has a new red and black shirt, and he looks perfectly dear! There's a little song, a sort of glad, wild song and yet—not so awfully happy—singing in my heart—I love you oh! I love you, my very dear!*

She was more than ready to fall in love. Pop, a transfer student from Storrs College in Connecticut, was a year older than Bill and four years older than Mother. He was six foot two and elegantly proportioned, with a dignified, proud face and strong, curved nose, generous lips, and thick, wavy, light-brown hair. He smoked a pipe and dressed fashionably in baggy knickerbockers (called plus fours) and oversized crewneck sweaters.

Pop's suave demeanor was belied by his stutter, which, he told me years later, came from having been forced, as a child, to write with his right hand instead of his left. But there had also been a lot of tension in his family life. His father, a dentist whose

ACTIVITIES

*A page from the 1928 Illio, the yearbook of
the University of Illinois at Urbana-Champaign*

Courtesy of the University of Illinois at Chicago, Library of the Health Sciences—
Chicago, Special Collections and University Archives Department

Pop and Mother, circa 1930

specialty was repairing the jaws of men who had been kicked by horses, was a binge drinker, unpredictable and violent; Pop told me of one occasion when he had had to call the police because his father had locked himself in the garage with a loaded shotgun.

Although Pop looked and acted like an intellectual, he did not do well in school, as I discovered when I sent away to the University of Illinois for my parents' transcripts. He failed to complete the work for a course in his major (landscape architecture) and got a D in seven others. Mother, however, earned honors in French, completed her education in three and a half years, and was admitted to the University of Illinois's graduate school in English.

In 1931, when Pop had graduated and returned to Connecticut but Mother was still at the university, she wrote him:

> Lover—and now, sweetheart, my lamb, it is I who must apologize—I haven't written you for two days—and I'm sorry, but I love you and love you anyhow. . . . I turned out the light, and hugged you very fiercely, because I loved you so much that I couldn't be very articulate about it. Sweetheart, how is it that I can keep on loving you more all the time, when already I'm practically bursting with it? But I do, you know. Maybe the "infinitely" accounts for it—because it is infinitely and always, beloved.

In October of that year—it was the midst of the Depression, and they did not get married until the end of 1932—Pop, twenty-four then, wrote Mother, twenty:

> Darling, there is something piteous and at the same time young and grand in the fact that the special stamp I shall affix to this letter will be bought with my last dime. The act seems to symbolize all sorts of struggle, young husband coming home lean-faced to his young bride every night walking on his socks and huddling over the little one after dinner, you know.

Two years ago Sunday, darling, we trembled so when
we got into bed that we couldn't lie still, and under your
left breast your heart was going so fast that it shook you.
My hands were warm, and yet when I touched you, you
jumped and quivered as if my hands were ice, and I
can still remember how fast you breathed and how your
breath felt against my cheek.

As the years—and there are enough of them now to
say "as the years go on"—with us as we concern each
other, there is a steadier, deeper quality of affection. But
it makes me afraid, a little, because it's such a sure sign,
inevitable, that we're getting older, and getting older
means getting old and then dying.

Mother left graduate school later that year to marry him in a small ceremony at the Episcopal cathedral of Hartford. She wore a blue-and-peach silk dress and jacket, telling me, years later, that she hadn't "deserved" to wear white.

In the forty-two years of Mother and Pop's marriage—the last year of which Mother was in the nursing home—they seldom argued. Mother usually deferred to Pop, even though, later, she might complain about him to me.

In 1963, Mother read Betty Friedan's *The Feminine Mystique.* Pop wrote to a friend that they had been reading together in the living room "like any pair of middle-years married folks, when she put down the book, looked across the room at me and said, 'I'd like to come over there and punch you right in the nose!'"

But she didn't. When Pop came home every night he would go at once to find Mother in the kitchen, embrace her, make a cup of instant coffee, and talk.

They had never been apart for more than a few days until Mother, at fifty-four, traveled to Amsterdam to see my oldest sister. Soon after she arrived, she wrote Pop:

Look, dolling, I'm a good-natured girl and a long-
suffering one you know, but this is a bit much. I started
looking for another letter a week ago, and now the mail
came and still nothing.

Mother, circa 1928

You really don't have to do one of those long conti-nued-a-week-from-Thursday things in your notebook. Just a few words scrawled on a postcard to tell me you're still around. I got so jittery the other night I almost called you. Now I'm mostly mad, but also still a little scared.

Since I've been here I've written you five long letters and to date I've had in return the letter you wrote the Sunday after I left. Period. All the new things and sight-seeing etc. are delicious and delirious, but it's still possible to get a little homesick, particularly at suppertime, which is the time everybody gets homesick if they're going to.

Pop wrote back:

I wish I could tell you in nice, glowing words how much I love you. I think one becomes inarticulate after so many years of loving someone in habit and complete trust. A hand-squeeze suddenly wanted can say more now than words ever did and I guess it's better, because we under-stand it so very well. I should have kept one of your hands.

She responded, "Your letter arrived yesterday. I know pre-cisely what you mean by no words. I do not deserve so dear a husband. I love you—unspeakably."

On Valentine's Day of 1973, only months before Pop put her in the nursing home, Mother drew hearts on a card and wrote him, "I love you for your understanding, I love you for your beyond-the-call-of-duty patience, but most of all I love you for your love."

A year and a half later, she was dead.

Pop was not without grief. Several months after Mother's death, when I was visiting him at Louise's vacation house, a piece of music that we had played in the days after she died came on the radio. Pop flung himself down next to me on the sofa, buried his face in my lap, and wept.

Pop moved in with Louise in her new house in California.

It was on a cliff with a spectacular view of the sunset over the Pacific. A Portuguese-tile stove warmed an enclosed sunporch, and there were brilliant bougainvillea bushes all around the backyard.

Louise was a good cook, and in the photos he sent, I saw that Pop had put on weight and acquired a suntan from long hours of reading outside. Even his silver hair seemed to be shinier than it used to be. But within two years, she asked him to leave. When, a long time after that, I asked her why, she replied:

> When your father owned his house and I owned mine
> we had a perfect time visiting each other. But once he
> sold his house to move out here, he never did anything.
> He had plans but never followed through. He'd get
> orders from libraries for the book-boxes and wouldn't get
> them done until the day after they were due. He drank a
> lot. I think he wished he didn't have to work.

Pop moved into a trailer park in a town not far from Louise's house. When I once came to visit him, I felt sorry to see him in this temporary, artificial community—without a store, or library, or town. The park seemed empty and lonesome—I didn't even see anyone outside. The few trees were short, lent no shade, and the bright sun beat down on the shiny metal roofs of row after row of trailers.

The town had an air force base and a federal prison. Pop had always liked old places with interesting histories—this town seemed like the last place he would ever want to live. Plymouth had been dubbed "America's Home Town," but this place seemed like nobody's.

Pop seemed delighted with the trailer, and pointed out to me all the features of the pale-yellow singlewide, including its Whirlpool appliances. The metal exterior of his trailer made it hot inside, and he had rigged up a complicated air-ventilator system that required mounting several shelves on the cardboard-thin wall of his living room, effectively cutting out much of the light and space.

I was reminded of what he had done to the porch of the Plymouth house. Because it had been built as a summer cottage

138

and was near the ocean, the house had a porch three-quarters of the way around it. Pop had wanted to turn the part of the porch that faced the ocean into a room that could be used in all seasons. But instead of using large panes of insulated glass, which he said were too expensive, he had installed small cast-off windows of different sizes, which he had scavenged at the dump. All of the wood in the window frames obscured the open view of the water. Then, because the enclosed room was too hot in the summer, he installed an air conditioner that effectively eliminated the ocean view once and for all.

Pop and I went grocery shopping. He was looking forward to my cooking for him—he had never learned to prepare more than boiled eggs and frozen dinners—and I made a stew of beef and vegetables, like the ones Mother used to make, so he would have some left over after I had gone home.

The second night of my visit, there was a storm with high winds, heavy rain, and radio reports of massive mudslides all over the state. I lay awake most of the night in the convertible sofa bed, the wall of the trailer's living room rippling behind me in the wind. I wished he would get out of there.

It was a relief, then, a few months later, when Pop told me on the telephone—stuttering, as always—that he had met Janet, a "n-n-nice w-w-widow," and, in another phone call soon after, that they were getting married. Janet's late husband had been a professor, and Pop was pleased that he, as her new husband, could assume the dead man's university club membership.

Janet had a magnificent house high in the hills with a wonderful view across San Francisco Bay. Pop described its charms with evident pleasure. Describing Janet, however, his voice was careful. He said that she was *n-n-nice*. I could not remember Pop ever having used that word to describe anyone he liked.

None of us children went to the wedding. They were married in her house, and he sent me a photo. It showed Pop and his bride, the minister between them, standing at a large picture window. Janet was looking at Pop, and Pop was looking at the view.

Over the next several years, Pop confided to me on the phone about his new wife's peculiar habits of thrift, especially notable in a woman who was, he emphasized, very wealthy. Janet saved used paper towels and pieces of tinfoil. She cut greeting cards she received in half and sent the unused half as a greeting card to someone else. She bought bruised, nearly rotten fruit. "She's had a f-f-few l-l-little str-str-strokes, you know," Pop said during one of his phone calls, and I could hear him lighting his pipe as he spoke. He did not say that he hoped she would die before him and leave him her money and the house.

Janet talked incessantly. Pop spent most of his time in his downstairs study, away from her, and slept in a separate room. Louise later told me that Pop had suggested to her that they resume their affair, but she had said, "It's not something I would ever do, so we talked on the telephone."

Janet and Pop had been married five years when Pop began to complain of constant aches in his arms. He became too tired to do anything. Then he forgot where he had left his raincoat. He forgot how to get out of a familiar building. When he told me on the telephone that he had been wetting his bed, and giggled, I flew out to see him, arriving at night.

In Janet's house, which I'd never visited before, when you looked out the front windows you felt you were flying. The lights of San Francisco over the inky blackness of the water were indeed spectacular. But the view was no longer of interest to Pop.

When I came to the door of his bedroom, which smelled of urine and looked like an interrogation or torture room in an old black-and-white movie, I saw at once that he was gravely ill. Lying in a narrow metal bed, he was staring into space. A battered old fluorescent desk lamp on a small table nearby cast a harsh, cold light on the floor. I had never before seen him lying down without a book in his hand. He brightened and greeted me affectionately, but showed no surprise at my sudden appearance there by his bed, late at night.

The next day, when Janet had gone out to get some groceries, I went into Pop's untidy study, sat down, and looked around. The rich blue Persian carpet, the handsome globe of the world in a carved wooden stand, the fine Italian-pottery table lamp,

Mother, circa 1918

and the gold fountain pen on Pop's cluttered desk had all belonged to Cornie's second husband.

Prominently placed on the wall above Pop's desk, in a dark wooden oval frame, was a photograph of Mother as a little girl, when she had been known as Tidie. Her long dark ringlets were topped by an oversize hair bow. Her eyes had a serious, melancholy look.

16

Returning

When I arrived at my gate in the Minneapolis airport, I looked around eagerly for my son, Sam, but he was not yet there. He was flying from New York to meet me, and then we were flying together to Mason City.

Sam had reached the age that I had been when Mother had died—twenty-eight. He was teaching high school history, and I was pleased that he was interested in his own family's past and was willing to go to Iowa with me. I had arranged for us to see the inside of the house in which Mother had grown up.

We planned also to visit the grave of his great-grandfather Sam and the graves of Cornie and her family. It was spring vacation, and although he had just returned from a brief trip to Europe to see his girlfriend, who was studying and working abroad, Sam had been willing to get back on a plane the next day to meet me here.

I wanted to be sure that I had shown Sam what Mother had not shown me. What Mother had not shown me was not just the town and the house in which she had grown up but how to live successfully. I did not want to die, as she had, without having given my son and my daughter a map of life that they might safely follow. I wanted to offer them the chance to learn from the mistakes of those who had gone before them—not only my mistakes but also those of previous generations of our family—so that they might not have to repeat them.

I thought I understood now why I had cried at my grandfather Sam's grave. Buried beneath that solitary, tilting stone was the love that Mother had been missing. And that I had been missing, too.

I hoped that my children would not have to search, as I had, for buried love. But it seemed that every child had to arrive at his or her own understanding of mother and father, and of all—good and bad—that they pass on.

Although I took out a book I was carrying and tried to read, I was unable to keep my eyes on the page for more than a moment. I was afraid Sam and I would somehow miss each other in the crowded waiting room. With only about thirty minutes to go before the plane was scheduled to depart for Mason City, my anxiety increased. What if he had missed his flight from New York? A lonely-seeming woman on my right, who was not reading but sitting idle, caught my eye as soon as I looked up, and began to complain to me about her long wait here for her plane. As I nodded, listening, a group of people entered the waiting area, and among them I saw a trim, six-foot-tall young man with dark hair, pronounced eyebrows, and a crease in one cheek, ambling along in an unhurried way. "Excuse me," I said to the woman, and, standing up, called out happily, "Sam!"

When I had named him, Mother had written to a friend, "Samuel was my father's name, and I am inordinately pleased by her choice."

After the short flight to Mason City, I signed for my rental car, Sam put our bags in the trunk, and we climbed in the front seats. The weather was cool and raw. It was the end of March, not full spring, no longer winter—that in-between time of year that in New Hampshire was called "unlocking season."

But the car would not back up, and I realized I had shifted it into neutral. This made Sam laugh. Both of my children liked laughing, and we enjoyed laughing together. As I sped down Route 18 to Mason City, we laughed again—we had left a trail of dust behind our car, like the cartoon character Road Runner.

After Sam slept—he had jet lag from his European trip—

we drove to a restaurant at one of the strip malls for dinner. I ordered a baked potato, which came with plastic tubs of I Can't Believe It's Not Butter (I could) and a triangular cardboard container with a black-and-white cow on it—when you squeezed it, sour cream was extruded like toothpaste. Sam and I looked at each other and laughed again—I had explained to him that Mother's grandfather had settled in Iowa because it was a superior dairy state. Over dinner, Sam told me about his trip to Austria. His description of Vienna as the city he would most like not to fall on him—so much of it was built of white marble—made me laugh.

Back at the motel, we turned in early. I liked having Sam on the other side of the connecting door between our rooms. For four years after he had been born, it had just been the two of us. Sam was the only member of my present family who had known Mother, although he had been only four when she died. He and I had shared experiences that my daughter, Kate, and my husband, Reg, had not. I had rarely had the chance since those early years to be alone with Sam.

Falling asleep, I heard the train whistle and remembered how I had imagined, on that first trip to Iowa, that it was the sound of a train taking me back to the past. But this time the whistles of a succession of trains annoyed me, sounding intermittently through the night. At one point in the still-dark morning, the loud sound jolted me awake, frightened, from a dream that the train was going to run into my room.

In the morning, while Sam got us coffee from the lobby, I turned on the television news, which invaded the morning with pictures and sounds of war, and with the faces of the injured and frightened American soldiers—somebody's Sams—who had been captured in a foreign country. I changed to the weather report.

I discovered that Sam and I had come to Mason City during highly unusual weather. There had already been a blue moon in January, and now, in March, there was another. The last time such a sequence of blue moons had occurred had been in 1915—when Sam, Cornie, and their little girl, Tidie, anticipating a happy future, had just moved into their newly built house. Now that same full, lovely, delicate globe that we had seen the previous night in the Iowa sky was shining down on us.

After our breakfast of cold cereal in Styrofoam bowls in the nook off the motel lobby, Sam and I drove off to Cornie's hometown, Charles City. It was thirty miles east on a straight road between flat fields, little to see but the leaden sky—the only surprise an ostrich farm about five miles outside of town. Nothing was green yet—fields were muddy, and a light rain drizzled down over the landscape.

We were looking for the site where Cornie's parents' graceful clapboard house—the "White house on the hill" had once stood, the home in which she had been born, and in which Mother had stayed when her parents left on that fateful night train in 1918.

I had seen a photograph of it in Cornie's album, its street address—812 Gilbert—written in white ink on the album's black paper. Sam and I found the address, circled back, and parked. Sam got out to stand on the spot where the house had been, beneath one of the two remaining elm trees, and gazed down at the Cedar River—the Wa-shood Ne-shun-a-ga-tah. I took a picture of him there. Would someone, yet unborn, look at this photograph someday, as I had looked at Cornie's?

I had not brought directions to Riverside Cemetery, where Cornie and her family were buried. "Let 'the force' take us there," Sam advised, in deep, exaggerated tones. But although the force got us quite near the cemetery, we did not find it until we had spent another half hour lost, and laughing about being lost, before we asked for directions. Later, I wondered whether we had laughed partly out of relief that neither of us, now, was lost, the way we had been when he was small and I was struggling to raise him alone.

But we figured out how to find our way. After we had driven into the cemetery, parked, and begun wandering among the graves, Sam found Cornie's family's stone. We stood together looking down at the spongy earth, at the slightly sunken stones engraved with the names of Cornie, Maude, Genevieve, Herbert, and Edna White. I did not think I would ever return. But Sam would know where they were.

Dark storm clouds began piling up in the sky, and we suddenly felt a little spooked. Back at the car, afraid for a moment that I had dropped the key somewhere among the graves, we shivered at the thought of being stranded in the cemetery in a storm. We both lived in cities and were used to seeing a lot of people around. Charles City seemed empty. Sam remarked that it was like "a ghost town," and we laughed wryly, since, for us, that's exactly what it was. I told him about the Winnebago belief that the spirits of their ancestors continued to occupy their burial grounds.

I had thought we might eat lunch at a tea shop I had noticed in an old building in Charles City—maybe my great-grandmother had once been in that building—but the speed with which the dark clouds were coming, our feeling spooky, and my dislike of driving in the rain made us decide to return to our motel. On the way, I asked Sam how he had felt about being in Charles City. "Strange. In a strange place, and yet connected to it," he replied.

Back at the motel, Sam went to take another nap, but I heard his phone ring, then his voice, and knocked on his door. It was his sister, my twenty-year-old daughter, Kate, away at college. When I told her we kept getting lost and laughing she said, "That sounds like fun! I wish I was with you!"

While Sam slept, I visited in the lobby with the local historian, who had stopped by to bring me some magazines featuring the Mason City houses designed by the architect Walter Burley Griffin, Sam and Cornie's among them. He told me that Miss Spooner, Mother's old teacher whom I had met on my first trip, had died. All these older people who were links to the past would be gone before long, and Mason City and Charles City would be entirely left to the younger people who had been brought up in the paved-over prairies. I was glad that I had been able to come and gather history while I still could, before all living links to Mother's time had been severed.

The next morning, in front of Sam and Cornie's house at 525 East State Street in Mason City, we read the marker in the sidewalk:

SAM SCHNEIDER HOUSE

1915

WALTER BURLEY GRIFFIN, ARCH. PRAIRIE SCHOOL

The present owners greeted Sam and me at the door and showed us through with obvious pride—the house had been near ruin when they restored it.

It didn't seem fair that Cornie's name had been left off the house's marker, because, according to an article that I had read in an architecture magazine, it had been she, the former art teacher, who, admiring the new Prairie school of architecture, had the idea to hire Walter Burley Griffin to design the house. Seeing the inside of it for the first time, my previous impression of her warmed. The house was not pretentious, but small, snug, and harmonious. Although it had been Walter Burley Griffin's design, Cornie had undoubtedly told him what she wanted.

The living room, dining room, and sunroom were on different levels, but each had a view of trees and grass and of the limestone cliffs of nearby Willow Creek. Those views, the cozy size of the rooms, and the unusual amount of daylight in the house—even on this gray day—gave it a feeling of serenity.

Upstairs, I entered the bedroom that, from architectural drawings I had seen at the Chicago Historical Society, I knew had been Cornie and Sam's. Looking at my reflection in the original full-length mirror on the front of the closet door, I imagined this same mirror reflecting Cornie, reflecting Sam, on that November day in 1918 before they had departed.

From the windows of the room that had been Mother's, there was a tranquil view of Willow Creek and of the trees. She must have sat here as she wrote in her diary. Looking out of her windows, it was as if, after all these years, I could actually see through her eyes.

Later we went to Elmwood Cemetery. Following the cemetery map, I drove to the correct section and parked. Sam got out and soon found the grave.

*Sidewalk marker in front of Sam and Cornie's house
at 525 East State Street in Mason City, Iowa*

(Griffin's name is misspelled)

Sam and Cornie's house

The view from Mother's girlhood bedroom window,
inside the house at 525 East State Street

So many years after the crushing sorrow of his unexpected death, here Mother's father still lay. Cornie, too, was ashes, and their child, my mother, also, now, ashes. But my Sam and I were here, remembering.

I had meant to bring flowers but had not seen a florist shop. I recalled the Jewish custom of placing a small stone on a grave as a sign that someone had visited and remembered. Sam searched around and found two stones, and we placed them on the gravestone of his great-grandfather. "That was a good idea," he said.

The next morning, Sam had to go home—he was tired from his travels to Europe and had a lot of papers to grade. A thunderstorm was on its way—the local weatherman called it a "thunderboomer"—and we hoped that his small plane could fly out. After a short wait at the clean, small airport, the time came to board. Sam's body when I hugged him had the high heat of youth.

I set off to drive to Garner, about twenty miles away, to meet a member of the North Central Iowa Genealogical Society who had found for me, in the archives of a local paper, the *Hancock Signal,* the obituary of my grandfather Sam's first wife:

> Died—At the home of her parents in Garner, Iowa, June 6th, 1902, of tuberculosis, Edith, eldest daughter of Mr. and Mrs. Elmer C. Abbey, and beloved wife of Samuel A. Schneider. She was born in Ellington Township, Hancock County, Iowa, December 18th, 1881.
>
> The above simple notice tells the story of the going hence of one who in this the home of her childhood was well beloved by all who knew her. On last Sabbath in a flower-ladened casket and amid the tears of mourning friends all that was mortal of "little Edie" was consigned to the silent tomb. On the threshold of womanhood— the bride of a few short months—she was called away from the family circle and the arms of a loving husband to enter the eternal abode of the heavenly father, and the sheltering arms of a loving savior, where she now awaits the coming of the loved ones who still linger on the shore of time.

Sam Schneider's grave, with the two stones
Sam and I placed on it

She is at rest, but our hearts go out in sympathy with the young husband as he treads life's pathway sorrowfully and alone, and for the remaining members of that family circle that has thus early been broken by the summons of the grim reaper whose name is death.

The obituary ended with a version of a poem by James Whitcomb Riley:

We cannot say, we will not say
That she is dead, she is just away!
With a tender smile and a gentle sigh,
She has gone to that fairer land on high,
And left us dreaming how very fair
It needs must be, since she is there.
We'll think of her still as the same and say
She is not dead, she is just—away.

After lunch at her farmhouse, the genealogist and I were going together to the cemetery where Edith had been buried. It was nearly the last remaining duty I felt in that place. I wanted to pay my respects to this young woman—only twenty when she died, the same age as my own daughter, Kate—who had been dear to my grandfather, and whose death, as it turned out, had made my own life possible.

When I knocked on the farmhouse door, the woman's delicate, wide-eyed six-year-old daughter followed her out shyly. "She's been asking and asking about when 'that lady' was going to come!" her mother said.

After our tuna casserole in the kitchen—the six-year-old, with a smile, said it was her favorite—we were off to Ellington Township Cemetery. The little girl scrambled happily out of the car. Her mother told me they had often searched through cemeteries, pursuing genealogy. The child skipped about among the tombstones, the hood of her bright pink sweatshirt pulled over her head in the gray day. The rain had slowed to a drizzle. "I love graveyards!" she cried.

As we approached Edith May Abbey Schneider's grave, a

robin sang—a sweet, hopeful, spring-is-here sound, despite the gloomy cold weather. A robin, a little girl in pink, her mother and I—all of us still "lingering on the shores of time." But Edith May Abbey Schneider had sailed away ninety-seven years earlier.

Her tombstone was engraved with her name and the words "S. A. Schneider's Wife." A tall marker with both family names stood nearby. As Edith's obituary had foretold, those Abbey family members who had once mourned her had eventually joined her, and were buried nearby. But her young husband, Sam, who had lived to marry another, then himself died too young, lay miles away, in a different cemetery. I left a small stone on Little Edie's grave.

Back at the farmhouse, a farewell and directions back, and then I scurried out in the suddenly heavy rain and drove away down the crunching gravel road, past the flat fields on either side—no houses, just the rain—until I reached Route 18, and a right turn, and hurried back to the motel, to the train whistle, to the next morning and my departure.

But I had one more thing to do that evening. The local historian, hearing my grandfather's name spoken by a woman at a dinner party, had learned that she was the daughter of Julius Kunz, that friend of Sam's who had gone to be with him at St. Luke's Hospital and who, with Cornie, had accompanied his body back to Iowa. Now in her late seventies, Julius's daughter had been born a few years after Sam had died.

She and her husband received me warmly at their home. She told me that her father and Sam had been close friends since childhood, and both had experienced the deaths of their first wives. Her father had not married again until he was forty. She said he had told her more than once about traveling down on the train to be with Sam when he was taken ill. He had driven her by Sam and Cornie's house to point it out to her. He had even wanted to name his first child Sam, but that child—herself—had turned out to be a girl. "Sam had many friends here," she told me. "My father said he was very well liked."

We had exchanged letters and photos before my trip. She had sent me a photo of her, at two, holding hands with teenaged Mother. And I had pictured her as that two-year-old, but of course she was an old woman now. For her, it seemed my presence was as surprising. She could not have expected that she would again meet anyone connected—even as remotely as I was—to her long-dead father. For both of us, talking about the old best friends—her father and my grandfather—brought them alive again.

She and her husband took me out to dinner. They probably felt sorry for me—far from home, pursuing facts about such a sad event so long ago. After dinner, we embraced and said good-bye. Their kindness touched me.

When I returned to my motel, my light was the only one on. It was silent on Sam's side of the connecting door. I ached for everything lost, and cried, over missing him, wishing that I could have made it possible for my children to have had only one father, no divorces; over my grandfather Sam's early death and the flower-laden coffin of his young bride, Little Edie; over Mother; over wars that took young soldiers' lives; over wandering around graveyards seeking something. When I was done crying, I called home and listened to Reg's sweet, deep voice.

Before I went to the airport the next day, I drove back to Mother's house and parked. I walked along East State Street, as she would have done, from her house to her high school. It had been new when she had attended; now it was no longer even a school— the sign over the door said CORRECTIONAL SERVICES.

Only a few steps farther stood what had in her day been the Carnegie Public Library. I stood at the entrance, remembering Mother's words in her diary, at fourteen: "Then we stopped at the library on the way home. Saw Kerm and he and I fought in a sarcastic manner. We hate each other cheerfully." It made me feel close to her to stand where she had stood, to feel the same sun on my face that had warmed hers.

17

Everything's Beautiful

The early-summer-morning clouds were pink. It was going to be another hot day. I had packed Mother's diaries, letters, and some of the photos of her as a child and young woman in my green canvas carry-on. I didn't want to entrust them to the airline in my checked bag.

I had awakened about five, had my tea, stirring it, as usual, with Cornie's silver spoon, engraved with the words "Charles City." I had just enough time, before the cab came, to bathe and finish packing.

The cab was prompt. At O'Hare, there was an hour's wait in line to check in, because so many flights had been held up by thunderstorms the previous day. I was grateful I had come early. Finally checked in and past security, I got coffee and walked through the long lit tunnel with its colorful neon to the far concourse. The sky was dark and there was lightning. But despite the plane being an hour late to board and another hour late taking off, I was content with my book, an absorbing mystery. Aloft, I enjoyed ginger ale and packets of crunchy cheddar crackers.

At the baggage claim in Boston, I heard a shouted "Cornelia!" and there was my old friend Linda. Since I had last seen her, her hair, like mine, had grown gray. Like me, she no longer looked young. But her face was still beautiful. Linda and I had become friends at sixteen, when Mother and Pop and I had moved to

Cornie's silver spoon from Charles City, Iowa

Plymouth. It was Linda who had said, remembering Mother, "I never knew anyone could have a mother like yours! I couldn't believe that she had memorized all of *Hamlet,* just for the fun of it."

Linda drove us out of the labyrinth of Logan Airport to Cambridge, to the Harvard graduate student dorm where we were staying that night. She lived on the Cape and had come up to accompany me the next day to the Arthur and Elizabeth Schlesinger Library on the History of Women in America, part of the Radcliffe Institute for Advanced Study and the Harvard Libraries.

I had been eager to find a permanent home for Mother's girlhood diaries from the 1920s, for her letters and the mementos Cornie had saved, for the photographs of three generations of women in my family. I wanted to preserve them so that other women might learn from and delight in reading Mother's diaries and these other personal papers of my great-grandmother and grandmother. I had also wanted to preserve my own diaries, written almost daily since I was thirty-six, which would be opened for anyone to read after my children's lifetimes.

The Schlesinger Library's mission was to document the lives of ordinary American women. The library had offered to take everything, and I had come to Cambridge to deliver Mother's diaries.

Linda and I found a garage, parked, rolled our bags to the dorm, huffed up two flights of stairs to our rooms, washed our faces, and changed into cool, clean clothes. We walked out to find dinner on Harvard Square. We hadn't seen each other much over the past forty years and had an endless amount to talk about.

The next morning it was clear but very hot, and after coffee and rolls in a café on Brattle Street, we walked down the street and across Radcliffe Yard, stopping outside the neat brick building with white painted trim that housed the Schlesinger Library.

I felt suddenly frightened. I had already taken back, from the little pile of papers I had packed, one of Mother's letters to me from the nursing home, unable, just yet, to relinquish it. Once I handed over her papers to the library, I would, finally, be leaving her behind.

My fear evaporated once I was inside the Schlesinger. It was cool, sunlit, quietly humming with women who were writing, reading, researching, and cataloging, like a hive of female bees. The curator took us to her office, where I took Mother's precious things out of my green canvas bag and explained each item, as she took notes. When we were done, she offered to take us on a tour of the library. As we left her office, I turned at the door to look back for a moment at Mother's things.

We descended into the basement archives, climate- and light-controlled rooms with shelves of carefully organized and orderly boxes of papers. The curator opened a cardboard box to reveal a gray plaster cast of a head and face—the feminist writer Charlotte Perkins Gilman's death mask. She opened drawers that contained posters and buttons from the women's suffrage movement.

When it was time to leave, I waited outside for a few minutes while Linda talked to the curator. As soon as I was alone, to my surprise, I began to sob. Mother was dead—she had been dead for so many years—but in the archives of the Schlesinger Library, that girl she had once been, described by Bill Maxwell as "brilliantly different and generally admired," would always be remembered. That girl who had written in her diary, at sixteen, of her boyfriend, "Oh, he's a sweet thing and I love him so—and I love life—and everything's <u>beautiful</u>!"

JANUARY 9 / 927.

Sunday again and a
simply perfect day!
With my Nathan
of course – Sunday
school and church in
the morning – breakfast
and then Nathan –
a good movie – chow
mein with mother & Nate
up to Riley's and home.
Oh – he's a sweet thing
and I love him so –
and I love life – and
everything's beautiful!

A page from Mother's diary, 1927

Courtesy of Schlesinger Library, Radcliffe Institute,
Harvard University, Cornelia Spelman Papers, 2003-M90, Box 1

ACKNOWLEDGMENTS

In loving memory of William Maxwell.

I am grateful for the many people who, over time, helped me as I was writing this book: Reginald Gibbons, Suzie Davenport, Linda Lee Doll, Charles D. Gelatt, Alane Rollings, Jeffrey Stewart, Muriel Benz, Maria Caserta, Richard Babcock, Christine Newman, Callie Warner, Alan Shapiro, Bruce Weigl, Angela Jackson, Kathleen Hill, Lesley Link, John Ellison, Jane Kaiser, Jean Estabrooke, Ruth Bittner, Katherine Faydash, Heather Antii, Marianne Jankowski, and Jenny Gavacs.

In Iowa, Terry Harrison, Art and Mary FIschbeck, Jari Sinnwell, June Kunz Gopelrud, Birdie Ellsworth, Gail C. Linahon, the Reverend Patti Aurand, the Reverend Kathryn S. Campbell, Phyllis Arthur, Sue Bier, Francis Holland, Gerald Edgar, Reta Spooner, Richard D. Scheerer, Marian Casey, Channing Dakin, the staff of St. John's Episcopal Church, Bill Harrold Realty, Ruth Umbarger, Jerry and Jo Kolpek, Mike Hummel, Helen DeSart, Robert E. McCoy, and the North Central Iowa Genealogical Society.

My thanks to the Illinois Arts Council for an Artist Fellowships Finalist Award in prose. I am grateful to the Lee P. Loomis Archive of Mason City History at the Mason City Public Library, Mason City, Iowa; the Charles City, Iowa, Public Library; the Newberry Library; the Chicago History Museum; the Ryerson and Burnham Library at the Art Institute of Chicago; the Rush University Medical Center Archives; Special Collections of the University of Illinois; the Milwaukee Public Library; Walter Burley Griffin Society of America; and the staff of the Arthur and Elizabeth Schlesinger Library on the History of Women in America.

Cornelia Maude Spelman, MSW, is the author of ten picture books for children, among them *The Way I Feel* series which help children recognize and manage emotion. Her books have sold over two million copies and been translated into ten languages.

www.corneliaspelman.com